Treating Late-Life Depression

LIBRARY

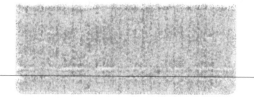

✓ **Treatments** *That Work*™

Treating Late-Life Depression

A COGNITIVE-BEHAVIORAL THERAPY APPROACH

Therapist Guide

Dolores Gallagher-Thompson • Larry W. Thompson

OXFORD
UNIVERSITY PRESS

2010

OXFORD
UNIVERSITY PRESS

Oxford University Press, Inc., publishes works that further
Oxford University's objective of excellence
in research, scholarship, and education.

Oxford   New York
Auckland   Cape Town   Dar es Salaam   Hong Kong   Karachi
Kuala Lumpur   Madrid   Melbourne   Mexico City   Nairobi
New Delhi   Shanghai   Taipei   Toronto

With offices in
Argentina   Austria   Brazil   Chile   Czech Republic   France   Greece
Guatemala   Hungary   Italy   Japan   Poland   Portugal   Singapore
South Korea   Switzerland   Thailand   Turkey   Ukraine   Vietnam

Published by Oxford University Press, Inc.
198 Madison Avenue, New York, New York 10016

www.oup.com

Oxford is a registered trademark of Oxford University Press

Library of Congress Cataloging-in-Publication Data
Gallagher-Thompson, Dolores.
Treating late-life depression : a cognitive-behavioral approach, therapist guide / Dolores
Gallagher-Thompson, Larry W. Thompson.
    p.   ;   cm. — (TreatmentsThatWork)
Includes bibliographical references.
ISBN 978-0-19-538369-0 (pbk. : alk. paper)
1. Depression in old age—Treatment.   2. Cognitive therapy.   I. Thompson, Larry W.
II. Title.   III. Series: Treatments that work.
[DNLM: 1. Depressive Disorder—therapy.   2. Aged.
3. Cognitive Therapy—methods.   WM 171 G162t 2009]
RC537.5.G355 2009
616.89′1425—dc22
                                                                2009010338

9   8   7   6   5   4   3   2   1

Printed in the United States of America
on acid-free paper

About Treatments *ThatWork*™

Stunning developments in healthcare have taken place over the last several years, but many of our widely accepted interventions and strategies in mental health and behavioral medicine have been brought into question by research evidence as not only lacking benefit, but perhaps, inducing harm. Other strategies have been proven effective using the best current standards of evidence, resulting in broad-based recommendations to make these practices more available to the public. Several recent developments are behind this revolution. First, we have arrived at a much deeper understanding of pathology, both psychological and physical, which has led to the development of new, more precisely targeted interventions. Second, our research methodologies have improved substantially, such that we have reduced threats to internal and external validity, making the outcomes more directly applicable to clinical situations. Third, governments around the world and healthcare systems and policymakers have decided that the quality of care should improve, that it should be evidence based, and that it is in the public's interest to ensure that this happens (Barlow, 2004; Institute of Medicine, 2001).

Of course, the major stumbling block for clinicians everywhere is the accessibility of newly developed evidence-based psychological interventions. Workshops and books can go only so far in acquainting responsible and conscientious practitioners with the latest behavioral healthcare practices and their applicability to individual patients. This new series, Treatments *ThatWork*™, is devoted to communicating these exciting new interventions to clinicians on the frontlines of practice.

The manuals and workbooks in this series contain step-by-step detailed procedures for assessing and treating specific problems and diagnoses. But this series also goes beyond the books and manuals by providing ancillary materials that will approximate the supervisory process in assisting practitioners in the implementation of these procedures in their practice.

In our emerging healthcare system, the growing consensus is that evidence-based practice offers the most responsible course of action for the mental health professional. All behavioral healthcare clinicians deeply desire to provide the best possible care for their patients. In this series, our aim is to close the dissemination and information gap and make that possible.

This therapist guide is designed to give mental health professionals the necessary tools to assess and treat depression, with or without accompanying anxiety, in the elderly. Designed specifically for use with older adults, the three-phase treatment described generally is delivered over the course of 16–20 sessions. Phase I provides an introduction to therapy, Phase II helps the client acquire the cognitive and behavioral skills needed to meet the therapy goals, and Phase III deals with termination and how to maintain the gains obtained in therapy.

Step-by-step instructions for administering therapy are provided in a user-friendly format, along with information on screening and assessment. Complete with sample dialogues, at-home assignments, and lists of materials needed, this comprehensive guide includes all the tools necessary for facilitating effective treatment.

David H. Barlow, Editor-in-Chief,
Treatments *ThatWork*™
Boston, MA

References

Barlow, D. H. (2004). Psychological treatments. *American Psychologist, 59*, 869–878.

Institute of Medicine. (2001). *Crossing the quality chasm: A new health system for the 21st century*. Washington, DC: National Academy Press.

Acknowledgments

We wish to extend our heartfelt appreciation to the numerous colleagues, students, and patients with whom we have worked and collaborated in our professional lives over the past 20 years. Their input has enabled us to develop, refine, revise, and update the materials and strategies included in both the therapist guide and the client workbook. We particularly wish to thank Dr. Aaron T. Beck and colleagues associated with the Academy of Cognitive Therapy for their support and encouragement—when no one else believed that CBT could be done with older adults, this group was there for us (and they still are!).

This research received major funding from several grants from the National Institute of Mental Health, and grants continue to be written to further study the efficacy of CBT with a variety of older adult patient populations. In addition, considerable support was provided by the Veterans Administration Health Care System located at Palo Alto, CA, and by the Department of Psychiatry and Behavioral Sciences of Stanford University School of Medicine.

Finally, we wish to thank our co-authors, Drs. David Coon, Leah Dick-Siskin, and David Powers, whose creativity and high levels of energy and commitment kept this project going during both challenging times and good times. They never gave up believing in the viability of CBT for depressed older adults, and never stopped maintaining effective collaborative relationships with us. For this we will always be grateful.

Dolores Gallagher-Thompson, Ph.D.
Larry W. Thompson, Ph.D.
Los Altos, CA, April, 2009

Contents

Chapter 1   *Introductory Information for Therapists*

Background Information and Purpose of This Program

The cognitive-behavioral therapy (CBT) program presented in this guide is intended for the treatment of depression, with or without accompanying anxiety in elderly individuals. The program draws heavily from the early work of Aaron Beck, Peter Lewinsohn, and their associates (Beck, 1976; Lewinsohn et al., 1985). Procedural modifications to various intervention strategies developed by these two groups—modifications that improve the applicability of these treatments in dealing with specific age-related problems and issues encountered when working with elderly clients who are experiencing notable psychological distress—have been the focus of our work. Over the past three decades, we have developed a number of empirically supported clinical protocols for use with specific symptoms or problems commonly experienced by the elderly, all of which embody the spirit and the methodology of traditional CBT models. The protocol in this book contains a single treatment program in which many of these variations have been integrated, along with appropriate comments detailing what kinds of problems and reactions to expect and suitable means to deal with them.

Late-Life Depression

Among the elderly, depression frequently results in increased (a) psychological distress; (b) impairment in behavioral functioning; (c) medical morbidity; and (d) economic hardship, especially in the later years. There is also an increased risk of mortality in depressed elderly patients who live in a nursing home setting or have a concurrent medical illness (Arfken, Lichtenberg, & Tancer, 1999; Black & Markides, 1999; Covinsky et al., 1999; Murphy et al., 1988; Rovner et al., 1991).

The prevalence of depressive disorders in late life has been a source of controversy over the past two decades. Much of the debate has been centered on methodological issues, such as exclusion/inclusion criteria, population sampling procedures, relevance of medical and physical problems, and so on. Detailed discussion of these and related issues is beyond the scope of this treatment package. Blazer and colleagues (Blazer, Steffens, & Busse, 2007) have provided a comprehensive discussion of these issues and their implications for establishing the epidemiological characteristics of late-life depression.

There is now a consensus among clinicians and clinical researchers that depression, however it is considered or whatever diagnostic scheme is used, is a common problem for individuals in their senior years. Conservative estimates suggest that more than five million seniors over the age of 65 are suffering from severe depression (see Koenig & Blazer, 2007, for a more detailed discussion of this literature). Furthermore, some methodologists argue that any current estimates are likely to be low, because our present assessment devices and criteria for classification of clinical disorders are not sensitive to the influences of age-related issues.

Since depressive symptoms are often associated with increased life stressors, it is understandable that the prevalence of depressive disorders would increase in the later years. Old age is a time of many losses—loved ones and friends, an occupation, finances, health, physical function, physical attractiveness, instrumental and supportive features of one's networks, and so on. Indeed, as one reflects on the magnitude of changes in the lives of the elderly, it's a wonder that more are not depressed. Over their life span, however, many have developed coping strategies to deal with such adversities. The resilience of many is remarkable, and they falter only when the problems accumulate to overwhelming proportions.

The implications of this pattern for treatment outcome can be quite positive for some individuals. Working with a client who has made successful adaptations through most of her life and then suddenly in the later years becomes overwhelmed due to the increase in negative life events can be decidedly different than treating a client who cannot deal with "life" because of characteristically poor adaptive capabilities.

Outcomes with the first type of client following professional interventions are often quite gratifying. It's not uncommon, for example, to have some older clients respond within a few sessions, maintain the improvements throughout the course of therapy, and show no evidence of serious relapse during follow-up, which in our program is approximately for 2 years. Others can be more challenging and require a more concerted effort to achieve improvements in depressive symptoms. In such instances, the addition of pharmacotherapy is often required. Pharmacotherapy alone can be very effective and commonly is psychiatrists' treatment of choice, particularly when psychotherapists are not readily available. For more severe cases, the combination of medication and psychotherapy is often recommended.

As will be seen later in this guide, appropriate assessment of the client's behavioral capabilities is pivotal in the development of an accurate case conceptualization and an effective intervention program. Because of the increased medical and psychosocial changes that occur in the older years, behavioral assessments can be more difficult to complete, but they play an even more important role in developing effective therapy strategies than with younger individuals. Because of this, Chapter 2 is devoted to a more detailed discussion of assessment issues and techniques.

Diagnostic Criteria for Depression

Table 1.1 lists the symptoms included in the *DSM-IV-TR* that are used for the classification of adult depressive disorders:

Table 1.1 Symptoms Used for Classification of Depressive Disorders

1. Depressed mood most of the day, nearly every day, as indicated by either subjective report (e.g., feels sad or empty) or observation made by others (e.g., appears tearful).
2. Markedly diminished interest or pleasure in all, or almost all, activities most of the day, nearly every day (as indicated by either subjective account or observation made by others).

continued

3. Significant weight loss when not dieting or weight gain (e.g., a change of more than 5% of body weight in a month), or decrease or increase in appetite nearly every day.

4. Insomnia or hypersomnia nearly every day.

5. Psychomotor agitation or retardation nearly every day (observable by others, not merely subjective feelings of restlessness or being slowed down).

6. Fatigue or loss of energy nearly every day.

7. Feelings of worthlessness or excessive or inappropriate guilt (which may be delusional), nearly every day (not merely self-reproach or guilt about being sick).

8. Diminished ability to think or concentrate, or indecisiveness, nearly every day (either by subjective account or as observed by others).

To meet criteria for *major depressive disorder*, the older adult must exhibit at least one of the first two (core) symptoms listed in the table (depressed mood and/or markedly diminished interest or pleasure in activities for the allotted time periods) plus at least four or more of the remaining symptoms included in the table. The criteria for *subsyndromal (minor) depression*, which appear in the appendix of the *DSM-IV* (1994), are still frequently used when diagnosing depression in the elderly. This diagnosis requires one of the first two symptoms combined with one to three of the remaining symptoms. *Dysthymic disorder* reflects more of a chronic condition and is also apparent in elderly clients, particularly those who are confronted with unrelenting medical, financial, or psychosocial stressors. The client must have depressed mood for most of the day, for the majority of days over a period of at least 2 years. While depressed, two (or more) of the other symptoms listed in Table 1.1 must be present as well. During the 2-year period, the client cannot be symptom-free for more than 2 months at a time and also should not meet criteria for major depressive disorder at any time during this time period. However, thereafter it is possible to have a major depressive episode superimposed on the dysthymic disorder and the client can meet criteria for both disorders.

Background of the Program

The development of this protocol was initiated back in the 1970s. At that time, only a few studies had been completed to evaluate the effectiveness of any psychotherapy with the elderly. In the Adult Counseling Center at the University of Southern California (USC), we saw a need for a structured treatment strategy to assist older adults in developing behavioral and cognitive skills to cope with their ever-increasing age-related life stressors. The two models we chose as the basis of our work focused on the reciprocal interaction of behaviors, cognitions, and emotions in the development of severe psychological distress. Beck and his associates (1979) had just recently developed and empirically evaluated cognitive therapy (CT), which focused on identifying and changing automatic dysfunctional thought patterns. Lewinsohn and his colleagues (Lewinsohn, Munoz, Youngren, & Zeiss, 1986) focused on behavioral therapy (BT), in which the treatment protocol is based on behavioral strategies designed to increase pleasant activities and decrease unpleasant activities in clients' everyday living conditions.

After numerous consultations and training visits with both camps, we initiated a feasibility study to evaluate the effectiveness of both in comparison to an insight-oriented relational therapy (IRT; Bellak & Small, 1965), which was the psychotherapy modality most frequently used in our center at that time. Ten clients diagnosed with major depressive disorder were randomly assigned to each of the three therapy modalities. They were seen for 16 sessions over a 3-month period and then followed up for 1 year. Therapists were advanced graduate students who were completing a segment of their practicum training. All were students in the clinical aging program at USC and had completed at least a full year of courses in Gerontology and Clinical Geropsychology. All sessions were taped for supervision purposes. Post-treatment improvement in depression was similar in all three treatment conditions, but follow-up evaluations indicated that clients in the CT and BT conditions continued to show improvement and maintained their gains across the 1-year interval, whereas the clients in the IRT modality did not.

Change over time in both self-report and interview measures were significant. There was no difference in the level of change between the BT and the CT conditions, but both showed significantly greater improvement than the IRT condition from pre to post treatment. At the 1-year follow-up, 27 of the 30 clients were interviewed and a clinical diagnosis was made. Only one patient of nine (11%), in each of the BT and the CT conditions was diagnosed as being in a depressive episode, while five of nine (55%) in the IRT condition were diagnosed as being in a major depressive episode (Gallagher & Thompson, 1982). Thus, 78% of the clients in the two structured treatments using a manual were symptom-free at 1 year following treatment.

This study was replicated with some modifications following a move to Stanford University School of Medicine and the Veterans Administration Palo Alto Health Care System (Thompson, Gallagher, & Steinmetz Breckenridge, 1987). Some of the modifications were as follows:

(1)   We were concerned that the differential effect between the structured therapies (BT and CT) and IRT may have been due to the absence of a manual for guiding the latter type of therapy, as well as the relative inexperience of the therapists (Crits-Christoph et al., 1991). So we included a more structured brief psychodynamic modality (Horowitz & Kaltreider, 1979) and recruited psychodynamic therapists trained by Horowitz and associates at the University of California, San Francisco, who also provided direct supervision of this group.

(2)   A 6-week delayed treatment control condition was added and a comparison between the delayed treatment and all therapy modalities was made at 6 weeks after therapy to rule out spontaneous recovery as a determinant of therapy success.

(3)   All therapists were postdoctoral psychologists with specialized advanced training in the specific modality they were delivering.

(4)   Videotapes of selected therapy sessions were rated by modality experts to determine if therapists were using appropriate intervention techniques. Clients whose therapist did not meet quality control standards in two of the taped sessions were to be

dropped from the study. None needed to be dropped because of this criterion.

(5)   The number of sessions was increased to 16–20 over a 3- to 4-month period to allow for scheduling problems and variable cognitive processing abilities in seriously depressed older clients. Finally, clients were followed over a 2-year period.

All clients ($N = 91$) were diagnosed by a research psychiatrist as being in a major depressive episode at the time they were randomly assigned to one of the four conditions. Both the Beck Depression Inventory (BDI) and the Hamilton Rating Scale for Depression (HAM-D) were obtained before therapy, at the 6-week point in therapy, after treatment was completed, and at select intervals over a 2-year follow-up period. Clients in all three treatment conditions showed significant improvement by the 6-week interval in treatment when compared to the delayed treatment control condition. Posttreatment evaluations showed significant improvement in depression in all three treatment groups across time.

Follow-up evaluations also showed no differences in the three groups (Gallagher-Thompson, Hanley-Peterson, & Thompson, 1990). At the end of treatment, 70% of each group had no clinical symptoms of depression or were substantially improved, while 30% were still diagnosed as being in a major depressive episode. At 1-year follow-up, 73% were symptom-free or had substantially improved, and 27% were still diagnosed as having a major depressive disorder. At the 2-year follow-up, these percentages had changed to 78% and 22%.

At 6-month intervals during the follow-up period, the Longitudinal Interval Follow-up Evaluation (LIFE; Keller et al., 1987) was used to determine the proportion of time clients were in a remission or a relapse. Again, no differences among the groups were observed, but there was a substantial degree of relationship between the diagnostic condition at the posttreatment evaluation and the proportion of time clients were in remission. Among those who were completely symptom-free at the conclusion of treatment, roughly 50% remained symptom-free from 18 to 24 months. Another 40% were in total remission for 13–18 months. The final 10% were in remission between 6 months to 1 year, and none were in remission for less than 6 months. Among those who were diagnosed with major depressive disorder, none were in remission for more than a year. Roughly 25% were in remission for 6–12 months, and 75% were in remission for less than 6 months. Nearly all of the clients in this group continued some type of therapy throughout the follow-up period. The group showing improvement, but with some residual symptoms, fell between these two extremes. Less than 10% were in remission for 18 months or more. Slightly more than 30% were in remission for 13–18 months. Slightly less than 30% were in remission for 7–12 months, and slightly less than 40% were in remission less than 6 months.

Thus, at this point, it was clear that 65–70% of older clients with a diagnosis of major depressive disorder had benefitted from structured short-term psychotherapy sufficiently to be considered in remission at 1- and 2-year follow-ups. Another 10% or so showed substantial improvement with only a few residual symptoms, leaving 20–25% who showed minimal change during treatment or follow-up, despite additional, and in some instances, aggressive therapies. It was also clear that those who responded extremely well and were judged to be symptom-free for 2 months or more were likely to remain symptom-free substantially longer than those who showed significant improvement but still had residual symptoms. In our judgment, these results were sufficient to dispel pessimism about the effectiveness of structured psychotherapies for treating elderly clients with major depressive disorder.

With these data in hand, we tried to determine what particular strategies in the three therapy conditions seemed to be most effective, and secondarily to determine if certain skill patterns could be associated with any particular individual differences. At the conclusion of therapy and at follow-ups, we had asked clients to rate the helpfulness of different skills they had learned, whether or not they were using them, and if so, how often. With regard to the first question we were able to identify treatment strategies that were more often rated as helpful, which also tended to be those that were used more often. However, we were able to link these with only a few factors reflecting individual differences, which we will discuss later. We then included the treatment strategies that were reported to be most helpful from all three conditions and used these with several clients in formative evaluation trials to determine how best to formulate a new manual combining both cognitive and behavioral techniques. After several iterations of this process, interspersed with focus groups involving the therapists using the new protocol and several clients who agreed to participate in the formative evaluation phase, we developed a CBT manual that has been the mainstay of our subsequent research and training efforts. It is our belief that this was one of the first CBT manuals to be developed for treating elderly clients suffering from moderate to severe depressive symptoms. We have used it in a major outcome study comparing CBT alone to the use of desipramine alone and a combination of the two. Additionally, we have used it for more than a decade in training clinical psychologists, social workers, psychiatry residents, and nurse specialists in mental health. Throughout this period, the manual has undergone only minor refinements to improve its appeal to clients and its effectiveness in helping clients develop (learn) new cognitive and behavioral skills to cope with negative situational stressors in their lives. As we have worked with therapists from different disciplines over time, efforts to simplify procedures have been introduced to make the manual more "consumer-friendly" for therapists, while also maintaining a rigorous structural package.

Our modified CBT manual was used in a randomized control trial comparing CBT to the medication desipramine alone and to a combined treatment package of desipramine plus CBT in the treatment of elderly clients diagnosed as being in an episode of major depressive disorder with mild to moderate levels of depressive symptoms (Thompson, Coon, Gallagher-Thompson, Sommer, & Koin, 2001). One hundred participants completed 16–20 treatment sessions over a 3- to 4-month period and then were followed-up for 1 year. Clients in the combined condition showed significantly greater improvement than clients in the desipramine-alone condition, but there was no difference between the CBT alone and the combined condition. Clients in the CBT-alone condition showed greater improvement on the self-report measure (BDI) than did the clients in the desipramine-alone condition, but not on the interviewer rating (HAM-D). Since some of the clients appeared to show a mild level of depressive symptoms, even though they were diagnosed as being in a major depressive episode, a secondary analysis was completed on clients whose HAM-D scores were in the moderate to severe range. Results were comparable on this subsample. Clients were further grouped according to the initial level of depression and the level of desipramine dose being taken. In the severe depression group that was taking a high dose of desipramine, the combined group had improved more than both desipramine-alone and CBT-alone groups. In summary, the combination of CBT and desipramine is more efficacious than desipramine alone in reducing depressive symptoms, but the efficacy of CBT alone over desipramine is less consistent in all the various analyses that were completed. Although the combined treatment was consistently more effective than desipramine alone in all of the analyses completed, it was more effective than CBT alone only in the subgroup of clients who were more severely depressed and were taking higher doses of desipramine. The data from this study provided more evidence confirming that psychosocial treatments can be effective in treating depression in older adults and need not be considered an adjunctive therapy or a second-line choice if and/or when medication cannot be prescribed.

Replications

The manual and training materials for this protocol have been available since the late 1990s, and they have been distributed to numerous VA Medical Centers and other tertiary medical centers throughout the country. The materials have also been distributed in the United Kingdom, where variations have been developed. Although these manuals or local variations are in wide clinical use, to our knowledge only two additional laboratories beyond our own have conducted randomized trials using this manual. Randomized clinical trials using this manual or some variation are listed here:

- Gallagher, D. E., & Thompson, L. W. (1982). Treatment of major depressive disorder in older adult outpatients with brief psychotherapies. *Psychotherapy: Theory, Research and Practice, 19*(4), 482–490.

- Thompson, L. W., Gallagher, D., & Breckenridge, J. S. (1987). Comparative effectiveness of psychotherapies for depressed elders. *Journal of Consulting and Clinical Psychology, 55*(3), 385–390.

- Gallagher-Thompson, D., Hanley-Peterson, P., & Thompson, L. (1990). Maintenance of gains versus relapse following brief psychotherapy for depression. *Journal of Consulting and Clinical Psychology, 58*(3), 371–374.

- Thompson, L. W., Coon, D. W., Gallagher-Thompson, D., Sommer, B., & Koin, D. (2001). Comparison of desipramine and cognitive behavioral therapy in the treatment of elderly outpatients with mild to moderate depression. *American Journal of Geriatric Psychiatry, 9*(3), 225–240.

Work in the United Kingdom

- Laidlaw, K., Davidson, K., Toner, H., Jackson, G., Clark, S., Cross, S., Law, J., Howley, M., Bowie, M., Connery, H., & Cross, S. (2008). A randomized controlled trial of cognitive behavior therapy vs treatment as usual in the treatment of mild to moderate late-life depression. *International Journal of Geriatric Psychiatry, 23*, 843–850.

Work in Alabama

- Scogin, F., Morthland, M., Kaufman, A., Burgio, L., Chaplin, W., & Kong, G. (2007). Improving quality of life in diverse rural older adults: A randomized trial of a psychological treatment. *Psychology and Aging, 22*, 657–665.

Since 1980, we have trained over 150 psychologists, psychiatrists, social workers, and nurse specialists using this protocol. Based on verbal report, we know that this protocol or parts of it have been used in many clinical centers as noted above. We have treated over 700 clients in our center over a 20-year period. We are also using modifications of the protocol to treat special populations, such as family caregivers in a group format. We have treated over 1,000 caregivers in the past two decades.

Population/Culture Specific Adaptations

Numerous ethnic minority depressed clients in our training and research programs have been treated using the original protocols with successful outcomes. Also in our laboratory, adaptations of this protocol for use with special populations, such as family caregivers, have been developed for Hispanic Americans, Asian Americans, African Americans, Persians, and males (specifically). Appropriate translations and back translations of the manuals and instruments for evaluation have been made, and randomized trials have shown the effectiveness of this technique in Latinos, Chinese, and African Americans (Gallagher-Thompson, Arean, Rivera, & Thompson, 2001; Gallagher-Thompson, Coon, Solano, Ambler, Rabinowitz, & Thompson, 2003; Gallagher-Thompson et al., 2007). This work is mentioned here because it suggests that if appropriate translations were made available and were being used by trained professionals who are bicultural/bilingual, there is little doubt that this protocol would be effective. It has been well received by numerous ethnic groups. This issue is discussed in a recent edited book entitled *Culturally Responsive Cognitive-Behavioral Therapy* (Hays & Iwamasa, 2006). Five of the authors in this volume trained in our center.

Recommendations for Program Implementation

Prerequisites

In order to use these manuals with maximum effectiveness, the person should have completed professional training, or at least be in the advanced stages of completion, in one of the clinical health–related specialties, for example, social work, clinical psychology, psychiatry, advanced nursing specialist in psychiatry or another behavioral specialty, or advanced occupational therapy. The critical component here is that in addition to having the requisite interpersonal skills, one must be familiar with the use of contingency models and have some appreciation of their utility in modifying behavior. In our experience, professionals who are not sympathetic to this position typically are not effective in using this protocol. However, often trainees are initially biased against the model, but after agreeing to try the techniques and experiencing their effectiveness, they become "converts" and proceed with further training with no difficulties.

The trainee should have knowledge about the problems and issues confronting the elderly and the general psychological, social, medical, and economic resources available to them that enable them to accommodate to life stresses. They should also have some experience in how to work with elderly clients, for example, regarding the strengths and weaknesses common to this group and how one uses this information in maximizing their potential for change. Sufficient information to fulfill this requirement can be obtained in two 3-semester hour courses—one for acquiring the basic information and one for sharpening interpersonal skills needed to work with this population. Courses of this nature are available online, sponsored by various professional organizations, so such information need not have been acquired in graduate school. We recognize that most clinicians do not have specialized training in gerontology, and this is not required—but is recommended—for the effective use of this protocol. The highly structured nature of the manual tends to offset deficiencies in the above areas.

Specific Training With the Protocol

We like to have trainees spend a year seeing clients using this protocol. However, actual progress in learning to use the manuals is negatively accelerated, that is, it is rapid in the early phase of training and less so in the later stages. Some trainees may have had an opportunity to acquire these skills as part of their professional training. Most trainees who come well prepared with appropriate background skills and specialized training can use the manuals quite effectively after working with 2 or 3 clients.

For those with a professional degree in mental health, a 3–6 month period of training should be ample to use this protocol effectively: 1–2 months for acquiring the necessary background and 3–4 months for individual supervision. Supervision can be done through review of audiotapes plus phone consultation. In some instances, more time may be required for skill acquisition. This would be worked out on a case-by-case basis.

Recommended Reading

Cognitive Behaviour Therapy With Older People by Laidlaw, Thompson, Dick-Siskin, and Gallagher-Thompson, 2003, Wiley: Chichester, West Sussex, PO19 8SQ, England, is an excellent reading source. This should be ordered directly from the West Sussex Office. We also have a behavioral training manual that is probably out of print, but feedback that we have got indicates that it is a good beginner's training manual. It is titled *Depression in the Elderly: A Behavioral Treatment Manual* by Gallagher and Thompson (1981), University of Southern California Press. The Library of Congress Catalog Number is 81-66766. ISBN is 0-88474-125-7. Finally, *Handbook of Behavioral and Cognitive Therapies With Older Adults*, editors Dolores Gallagher-Thompson, Ann M. Steffen, and Larry W. Thompson, 2003, New York: Springer Publishing Co., provides substantive material on the use of CBT variations with a wide range of clinical disorders.

For those who have had minimal exposure to cognitive and behavioral techniques, we recommend a book by Judith Beck titled *Cognitive Therapy, Basics and Beyond*, 1995, Guilford Press, and *Control Your Depression* by Peter Lewinsohn and his associates, 1986 (2nd edition), Prentice Hall. There are any number of excellent books in this area which cover the same basic material. We think these are less costly and used copies are often available.

CBT Model of Depression in the Elderly

Our model for CBT of depression in the elderly calls attention to the importance of supplemental contextual information. In older clients, there are typically numerous substantive changes in relevant psychosocial and physiological processes that can influence strategies used in therapy, more than with younger clients. The diagram of the CBT model included here in Figure 1.1 highlights the importance of this

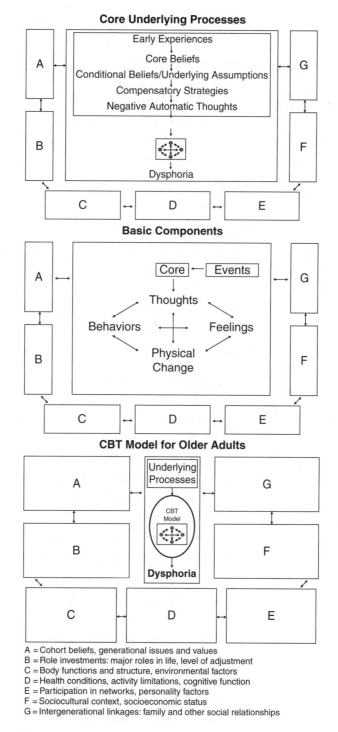

Core Underlying Processes

A

Early Experiences
↓
Core Beliefs
↓
Conditional Beliefs/Underlying Assumptions
↓
Compensatory Strategies
↓
Negative Automatic Thoughts

G

B

F

↓
Dysphoria

C ↔ D ↔ E

Basic Components

A

Core ← Events
↓
Thoughts
Behaviors ↔ Feelings
Physical Change

G

B

F

C ↔ D ↔ E

CBT Model for Older Adults

A

Underlying Processes
CBT Model
Dysphoria

G

B

F

C ↔ D ↔ E

A = Cohort beliefs, generational issues and values
B = Role investments: major roles in life, level of adjustment
C = Body functions and structure, environmental factors
D = Health conditions, activity limitations, cognitive function
E = Participation in networks, personality factors
F = Sociocultural context, socioeconomic status
G = Intergenerational linkages: family and other social relationships

Figure 1.1

CBT Model for Older Adults.

information. The case conceptualization illustrated in the first segment highlights the Core Underlying Processes; this critical component must be well formulated early in the therapy process for CBT to be maximally effective. A major part of case conceptualization is to identify various core beliefs, conditional assumptions, and compensatory strategies that might be related to the client's expressed problems. It is usually not possible to complete the conceptualization in the first session itself. Rather, throughout the early phases of the treatment, the therapist is gleaning information that will help her or him complete the conceptualization component.

As noted in the second part of the diagram, labeled as Basic Components, the impact of the core beliefs influences the negative automatic thoughts that occur in the face of a stressful event. These in turn affect feelings, behaviors, and physiological changes. All of these basic components can also reciprocally affect one another and lead to an escalation of negative thoughts and feelings, resulting in a clinical condition of dysphoria.

The final segment of the diagram is intended to emphasize the relative importance of other contextual influences on the development of clinical disorders in the elderly compared to the young. When working with older adults, it is critical to evaluate various aspects of these influences. As noted in section **A** in Figure 1.1, the experiences of different cohort groups lead to shared beliefs and values that may vary across age groups. Thus, for example, individuals who suffered during the Great Depression are likely to have different concerns about economic factors than individuals of the baby boom era. Similarly, role investments (**B**) are often different for different cohorts and can change across the life span. In older cohorts, males are often valued as the major provider and decision maker, while females are viewed as being supportive and involved in homemaker activities. In later years, circumstances may lead to a reversal of these expectations. Thus, the male is no longer the breadwinner and must find elements of self-worth and value in other activities. Also compromises and negative changes in how their bodies "work" are common in the elderly (**C**), which makes it difficult for them to function effectively and maintain autonomy and independence if the living conditions are not supportive. Functional impairment is often related to health conditions (**D**), which may need medical attention. In addition, older adults may or may not participate in satisfying social networks (**E**), which may be due, in part, to long-standing personality features (such as being introverted compared to extroverted). Their ability to have a good quality of life is also affected by socioeconomic status (**F**) and by their "connectedness" (or lack thereof) with family, friends, and the "younger generation" (**G**).

In order to develop a comprehensive case conceptualization, we recommend that each of these areas be assessed—either formally (using appropriate questionnaires) or informally (by interviewing the client, family members, if available, and other health care providers). Informed consent should be obtained as soon as possible so that communication with the primary care physician (PCP) and other relevant allied health care professionals can occur (e.g., social worker, clinic nurse, physical therapist, occupational therapist). Additional discussion concerning these contextual features will be presented in Chapters 2 and 3.

Risks and Benefits of This Treatment Program

There have been no adverse effects of any substance in any clients while they were enrolled in treatment programs for clinical research or training in our center. Over the years, less than 10% of clients receiving CBT or a combination of CBT and pharmacotherapy have required outside consultation because of increasing symptoms. Nearly half of these were more distressed because of deteriorating medical conditions. Six other clients were hospitalized for more intense inpatient psychiatric treatment.

The benefits are most often very encouraging, as noted in earlier discussions focused on treatment evaluation. Looking at the overall summary of clients involved in our research and training programs, approximately 67% of the clients we have treated with CBT alone have shown substantive improvement, and nearly 60% were classified as being in complete remission with no major clinical symptoms at the conclusion of treatment. The remaining clients either showed no change over the course of 12–20 sessions and a 1-year follow-up (12%), became worse during the initial protocol and required more aggressive treatment (roughly 7%), or experienced intermittent improvement and decline over the course of therapy and follow-up (14%).

Alternative Treatments

Traditionally, pharmacotherapy has been viewed as the first line of treatment for severe depression in the elderly, and psychotherapy has been considered an adjunctive treatment. However, more recent treatment guidelines emphasize that both are recommended for major depression, dysthymic disorder, and minor depression (Blazer, 2003). Several forms of psychotherapy are known to be effective in treating geriatric depression. Interpersonal psychotherapy is also frequently used with this population (Frank, Frank, & Comes, 1993; Frank & Spanier, 1995). Brief psychodynamic therapy, developed by Horowitz and Associates (Horowitz & Kaltreider, 1978; Marmar, Horowitz, Weiss, Wilner, & Kaltreider, 1988), is effective and has been used frequently in treating clients undergoing severe stress, such as bereavement. Other common treatments used, which are actually considered variants of CBT, include dialectical behavior therapy, used with elderly clients with personality disorders (Cheavens & Lynch, 2008), and problem-solving therapy (Bruce et al., 2004), used frequently for depressed clients in primary care settings.

Outline of This Treatment Program

Generally, the protocol we use for depression takes about 16–20 sessions, depending on how quickly the client can learn the particular skills or strategies being worked on in therapy sessions. As commonly found in other CBT models, this therapy has three phases: The first phase is loosely referred to as "socializing the client into therapy" and usually takes anywhere from 1 to 3 sessions. During this period, the therapist elicits several primary complaints the client has and then works collaboratively with the client to develop therapy goals that address the client's complaints. The client is also informed about the techniques used in therapy and what she can expect to see happen. Emphasis is placed on describing the client's role and responsibilities during the course of therapy, as well. The second phase is the longest and focuses on helping the client acquire the cognitive and behavioral skills needed to meet the therapy goals. The final phase focuses on termination and how to maintain the gains obtained in therapy. Clients develop a "survival guide" to remind them of what skills can be most helpful in various stress-producing situations that are likely to occur. We also recommend that sessions be spaced further apart to let the client have the chance to become less reliant on the therapist and therapy sessions. And finally, a couple of booster sessions at intervals of several months following therapy can facilitate continued use of skills and thus minimize relapse rate.

Further description of the early, middle, and late phases can be found in the introduction to each phase included in this manual. Specific modules in this guide include outlines of recommended elements and detailed instructions for conducting the therapy with older adults. Table 1.2 provides a recommended structure of therapy sessions for older adults.

Table 1.2 Recommended Structure of Therapy Sessions for Older Adults

---

- Prior to session, have client complete a monitoring assessment form to track progress on specific target, e.g., mood, anxiety, select activities.
- Do a mood (symptom) check, including review of self-report form.
- Set the agenda collaboratively for the session.
- First on the agenda is always **Review home practice**.
- Identify a treatment goal to be the focus of the session.
- Select an appropriate cognitive or behavioral strategy to address the goal and work on the steps of learning to apply the skill, including role playing and completing thought records.
- Have client summarize to determine level of understanding.
- Review rationale for the strategy, and develop next home practice assignment; problem solve barriers.
- Summarize and obtain feedback on the session.

The client workbook that corresponds to this manual is an integral part of the treatment.

Therapists will want to refer to the workbook for case examples that demonstrate the relevance of the therapy for older adults. The workbook also provides forms for the client to complete and therapists will want to review these with the client in session. Thus, it is recommended that therapists keep a copy of the workbook for reference and that clients bring their workbooks to every session. At the end of each session, therapists will assign home practice as appropriate.

Chapter 2   *Assessment of Older Adults*

Introduction

Assessment of cognitive, emotional, and functional status is recommended prior to beginning CBT with an older client. This provides a clearer understanding of the client's main problems *and* enables the therapist to determine whether or not the client is a suitable candidate for CBT. It is usually possible to obtain only a brief psychosocial and psychiatric history, some information about medical status, and administer a few screening measures during the 60–90 min appointment. So it is important to remember that this screening, on multiple levels, is not equivalent to finalizing a diagnosis! Screening typically can lead to further detailed workup by appropriate professionals if necessary, including the following:

- Medical and laboratory studies (e.g., if depression symptoms are present, but appear to be strongly related to a possible medical disorder)

- Detailed psychological or neuropsychological assessment (e.g., if the client appears demented, further cognitive assessment should be done to determine the extent of the cognitive impairment)

- Analysis of social resources available (e.g., if the client appears to have functional limitations and minimal instrumental and emotional support, referral to a social worker or other professional to assist in obtaining required community resources)

- When time and resources permit, evaluation of all areas outlined in the CBT model for older adults shown in Figure 1.1 in Chapter 1. Questions to consider for assessment reflecting components of the model are listed later in this chapter.

Since most clinicians do not have a great deal of time to spend on this, we will also briefly present recommended measures, their rationale for inclusion, and where to find them for the following essential areas of assessment:

1. Cognitive function/mental status

2. Substance abuse

3. Levels of depression and anxiety

4. Suicide ideation/hopelessness

5. Medical history/current problems/disabilities, functional impairments

6. Social supports and other domains indicated in Figure 1.1

Preparing for the Assessment: Things to Consider

First, we want to review several basic issues critical to obtaining an unbiased assessment of the client's functional capabilities. When scheduling the assessment interview, it is important to remind the client to bring his glasses and/or hearing aids and any other devices or supports that he needs in order to spend 1–2 hours responding to your questions. Diabetics, for example, may need to bring juice or special food to eat if they experience a drop in blood sugar; many older adults (especially those on multiple medications) need to bring water and their pills with them, so that they can remain "on schedule" with their medication regimen. It is *always* a good idea to ask the client to bring all of his medications with him, preferably in their containers, so you can see for yourself what they are and what doses are supposed to be taken, when. If this is not feasible, ask the client to bring a list of medications: name, dose, time to be taken, and what each drug was prescribed for. Finally, it is a good idea to ask the client to bring the name, address, and phone number of his primary care physician and any other specialists with whom there is regular contact, so that you can ask the client to sign a release of information permitting you to communicate with the medical team. If the client wishes to bring a family member to the appointment, we generally agree to that since the client may be unreliable in giving his own history. Also, the family member can often present multiple aspects of the problem, from his or her perspective, that can be informative for therapy.

At the time of the appointment, remind the client to use his assistive devices. Ensure that the testing area is reasonably quiet, free from distraction, and has a comfortable workspace (e.g., desk or table for writing) that has sufficient light. Evaluation can be threatening to older adults, particularly those with little formal education and/or evidence of at least mild cognitive impairment. So it is helpful to reassure the client that the reason you are doing this is to enable you to develop a better, more effective treatment plan for the therapy.

Ask the client how he wishes to be addressed: Many prefer formal titles such as "Mrs." or "Mr.," or "Dr." if that is appropriate. They often wish to call you "Dr. so and so" and not use your first name (as a sign of respect). Also ask if the client would prefer to have the family member in the room or not; in cases where a family member accompanies, it's generally good to begin with the family member there, and then at some point to ask the client if he would like to have an individual, private interview. This is generally the case once the "formal" assessment procedures are initiated. Family members are most helpful for obtaining an accurate history, but are very distracting once evaluation measures are being administered. If they remain in the room, they often answer "for the client," which is not what you are after.

Client's Ability to Focus

The assessment will require the client to focus; therefore, it is important to consider the following:

- Does the client seem able to focus on the tasks, or is he very distractible? That should become evident during the history-taking portion of the session.

- Is the client too distressed to focus or concentrate on completing test items? Some very depressed clients are too tearful, or anxious, to really complete the entire evaluation in one appointment.

- Is there evidence of delirium? Delirium, while not common in outpatients, it can be recognized by a sudden change in level of consciousness and ability to process information. If it is suspected, referral to the client's primary care physician, or to an emergency care facility, is the best course of action. Clearly, in such cases, evaluations of cognitive and affective status should be delayed.

Referral Question

It is important to keep the referral question in mind when conducting the assessment. Was the client referred by his primary care physician (PCP) for treatment of depression, specifically? Or, was the referral more general: e.g., to rule out depression or dementia? Was the client self-referred? Typically, clients are referred by a PCP, another medical professional, or come at the request of a family member. Often, they do not really know *why* they are seeing you, and you may need to provide an explanation.

CBT Model for Older Adults: Psychosocial and Health Factors of Importance for Case Formulation

The conceptual model presented in Chapter 1 (Figure 1.1) highlights the importance of psychosocial and health factors in seven different areas. Many of the factors listed could be relevant for case formulations with clients of any age. However, these all have added significance when working with the elderly, because they typically show more extreme variations than in other age groups. Older individuals who are experiencing depression and/or anxiety invariably are experiencing problems in one or more of these areas, and they all need to be considered very carefully when formulating a therapy plan with clients in this population. Detailed discussions of their importance are included in our earlier reference on CBT with older adults (Laidlaw, Thompson, Dick-Siskin,

& Gallagher-Thompson, 2003). A brief discussion of these is provided in the following sections, followed by Table 2.1, which lists several relevant questions in each area to consider during the assessment.

A: Cohort Beliefs/Generational Issues and Values

It is often the case that the therapist working with an older client is much younger and from a different age cohort. The shared beliefs of one age-specific generation are much different than those of another, by virtue of their shared experiences. Thus, elderly individuals who suffered through the Great Depression will usually have different economic concerns than baby boomers. Many find the beliefs they developed during their formative years are no longer functional, which can cause considerable stress. Attitudes toward therapy also are usually different at the start of therapy. Some believe that evidence of psychological distress is a sign of weakness and an inability to cope with the stresses that arise in their lives. They may feel that a need to seek help is evidence of weakness that they do not want others to see. Some may believe that therapy is ineffective, and they are coming only because their PCP or family members applied pressure to do so. Having no experience with talking therapy as a treatment modality, some may simply have no idea what to expect. The therapist will need to explore the beliefs and attitudes of the client early in an attempt to dispel any erroneous concerns the client may have about discussing his personal problems or the futility of psychotherapy as a treatment modality.

B: Role Investments

One of the important ways that individuals validate self-worth is through the roles they are involved in during their lives. As individuals enter the late adult years, it is often necessary for them to transition into new roles which may not offer the self-validation of earlier roles. For example, a man who has always valued his worth most importantly from his job and the financial support he provided for his family may have difficulty valuing his worth or contributions during retirement. A woman who as a result of her husband's illness has had to change her role from that of a caring supportive family member to the head of the household may find the stress unbearable. Therapists need to take the time to explore past role investments to determine how they have changed as the client has transitioned from one developmental phase to another and what the implications of this might be for how the client now values himself and his contributions to his family and community.

C: Body Functions and Structure—Environmental Factors

Careful attention must be given to the client's ability to function independently in his current environment. Can the client manage his own care? If not, why not? Is the problem due to his current mental or physical condition? Can it be remedied through therapy to increase independence? Are there limitations within the environmental setting that could be changed to foster independence? What specifically requires modification? Are there specific issues that can be dealt with in therapy to facilitate independence and autonomy? Assuming this can be achieved, are there other strategies needed to improve the client's level of distress?

If the client's present functional impairment and environmental support systems cannot be changed, then the formulation for therapy from the beginning will likely emphasize the exploration of possible serious distortions based on accurate negative appraisals and subsequent intense levels of depression and anxiety. Once these are identified and challenged, use of cognitive reframing and acceptance may become the focus of the therapy work.

D: Health Conditions—Activity Limitations

Older adult clients who come for therapy often have accompanying medical problems, and many have dysfunction in multiple systems. As noted in Chapter 1, prevalence of depression is substantially higher in clients with medical problems, and the prognosis for improvement in chronic medical conditions is lower in individuals who have depression. When depression remits, prognosis for medical conditions also generally becomes more favorable. Careful attention is called for in clients who have medical complaints, and if possible, consultation with the client's primary physician or other medical specialists is recommended. Adjustments in therapy procedures may be called for because of health problems. If pain is sufficiently intense to interfere with function, specific therapy strategies to help individuals deal with pain and increase activity levels may facilitate progress in therapy. Some clients who have medical problems view their depression as a medical problem and therefore believe that only medical treatment can alleviate the distress. In such instances, usually little progress can be made until the client entertains the notion that psychological distress is not necessarily due solely to a physical condition.

E: Participation in Networks—Personality Factors

The late adult years are a time of loss, and social networks are not spared. Friends and family die or move from the area. Many communities have few organized institutional support systems, or even if they do, elderly persons with depression tend not to use them. Usually, at a time of transition brought on by loss of a spouse or a job, development of serious medical problems, inability to maintain a large home, or other such instances, the older person may leave an established network with the expectation that the move will improve his situation, when in fact it actually increases his level of distress. Generally, individuals of all ages often fail to appreciate the importance of community networks to their general well-being, or they have unrealistic expectations about the time and effort it takes to develop a new community support network.

Whatever the reason, leaving an established network system increases the risk for the development of depression. This is particularly apparent in situations where a parent moves to a new area to be near his adult children. Because there is no community network, the parent must rely solely on the children for support. The children frequently have obligations to their own family, job, and community and are not comfortable in assuming the additional responsibilities of caring for a parent. This can sometimes cause serious stress in the parent–children relationship, and the parent often senses rejection by the children. So, not only did the parent lose his established community network, he also now feels that he is being rejected by his children.

Personality factors can also affect the development and maintenance of a strong supportive network, either positively or negatively. Individuals who are extremely rigid in their interactions with others, or otherwise have a personality disorder, have difficulty establishing and maintaining a network. For individuals with high resilience, flexibility, and good interpersonal skills, the task is usually less daunting, but as noted previously, it is often tedious and takes time even for mentally healthy individuals to develop new social networks from scratch. If they are experiencing other serious stresses at the same time, then the cumulative effect may put them at risk for the occurrence of a depressive disorder.

F: Sociocultural Context—Socioeconomic Status

This refers to several important influences that shape how a person tends to see the world. First is the socioeconomic status (SES) of the individual's family during his childhood and adolescence. For example, many adults now in their 60s and 70s grew up in rural areas or very small towns, where educational opportunities were limited.

Besides SES, the client's "context" or background includes his religious upbringing, values and beliefs that were commonly held in the family. Transition to new social systems in adulthood may confront the client with contradictory value systems. For example, if the client is a first-generation American, he had a different experience growing up compared to clients whose family is third-generation American, and so on. Discovering salient facts about the client's sociocultural context will help the therapist understand early influences that shaped his world views and belief systems. Many of these may still be affecting the client today, although he may not be aware of this.

G: Linkages Connecting Elders With Their Social System and Culture

Older adults generally have complex family relationships. Although divorce was not common in their era, they may have been married more than once and so may have children from more than one marriage. Thus, there can be complicated in-law and step-child relationships. At the present time, they may be widowed, divorced, or separated, and possibly living alone, with a companion or friend, or with one or more of their adult children and/or grandchildren. It is therefore important to inquire about marital history and if widowed, separated, or divorced later in life, what the circumstances were. Often, relationships with the spouse (if still alive) are a mixture of positive and negative aspects; the same is generally true with adult children. If there are several children, the older client usually gets along well with one or two and is more distant from the others. If the client is dependent financially, or for physical care, on one of the adult children, that also changes the nature of their interaction. We have also noted that most older clients who are depressed have few, if any, friends, and have dropped most or all of their normal social activities (clubs, church attendance, senior center outings, etc.). Thus, the social network tends to be both constricted and conflicted.

Although consideration of all the components of the CBT model for older adults is recommended, due to time or resource constraints, clinicians may choose to focus their assessment on essential areas.

Table 2.1 CBT Model for Older Adults: Questions to Consider

A. Cohort Beliefs/Generational Issues and Values
- What are the shared beliefs and experiences of an age-specific generation?
- What are the economic concerns common to an age-specific generation (e.g., elderly who suffered the Great Depression vs. the baby boomers of the dot-com era)?
- For clients who are veterans, what are the common fears for their generation (e.g., Agent Orange vs. road bombs)?

B. Role Investments
- How are major life roles different for different cohorts and how do they change differentially with age? (E.g., for older cohorts in earlier years, males are valued as the major provider and decision maker and females are supportive and maintain organization and structure. In later years, expectations may reverse.)
- How do role investments influence the client's level of adjustment?

continued

Table 2.1 CBT Model for Older Adults: Questions to Consider *continued*

C. **Body Functions and Structure—Environmental Factors**
- Can the client function independently in his environmental setting?
- Does the client have autonomy?
- Does the environment help or hinder independence and autonomy?
- What factors require modification to promote independence and autonomy?
- What specific treatment interventions might facilitate independence and autonomy?

D. **Health Conditions—Activity Limitations**
- What are the major health concerns that impact on therapy?
- What is the client's level of pain?
- What are the client's activity constraints?
- Are there any medical problems provoking caution and constraint?
- Are there any medical alerts and required adaptations?

E. **Participation in Networks—Personality Factors**
- What types of formal instrumental and emotional support networks are available?
- Has the client been able to benefit from either instrumental or emotional support systems?
- If not, what are the barriers?
- Are personality factors important determinants? (e.g., resilience, flexibility, openness to new experiences, or Axis-II personality disorders)
- How can these factors be addressed in therapy?

F. **Sociocultural Context—Socioeconomic Status**
- What are the beliefs about aging and the elderly in the client's community?
- How are these likely to affect the client's ability to change present behaviors?
- What strategies might offset any sociocultural problems?
- Are the client's economic resources adequate to minimize negative societal effects of ageism?

G. **Linkages Connecting Elders With Their Social System and Culture**
- Are there identifiable persons or systems that can facilitate the client's reintegration into his social network?
- Are mechanisms in place to facilitate the utilization of formal health and/or economic services?
- If competency is an issue, are social and legal professionals available to implement relevant level and type of power of attorney?
- How will these issues affect the course of therapy?

Assessment of Cognitive Function/Mental Status

Cognitive function or mental status is a critical area for assessment due to the significant impact it can have on the client's overall functioning—particularly on his ability to participate in, and benefit from, CBT.

Mini-Mental State Exam

The most commonly used screening tool for cognitive function/mental status is the Mini-Mental State Exam (MMSE; Folstein, Folstein, & McHugh, 1975). The MMSE is an 11-question measure that tests five areas of cognitive function: orientation, registration, attention and calculation, recall, and language. The maximum score is 30. A score of 23 or lower is suggestive of cognitive impairment (although in some instances, other factors may be responsible for poor performance, such as anxiety or low education). The MMSE takes only about 10 min to administer and is a useful screening measure, but should not be used to formulate a diagnosis (Tombaugh & McIntyre, 1992). It has been used extensively in both clinical practice and research over a quarter century (see Lezak, 1995, for review and commentary on the appropriate use of this scale). The MMSE is now copyrighted and must be purchased from Psychological Assessment Resources (PAR) in Lutz, FL. Note that it is useful to consider norms based on age and educational level (Crum, Anthony, Bassett, & Folstein, 1993) to minimize false positives in persons with low education. False negatives occur most often in clients with high educational levels.

Clock Drawing Test and Other Alternatives to the MMSE

For clients with low literacy or for whom English is not their primary language, use of the Clock Drawing Test should be considered. The client is given a blank sheet of white paper and a pencil and asked to draw the face of a clock with all the numbers on it (using either Arabic numbers or Roman numerals) and then set the hands at 20 to 4. See Tuokko, Hadjistavropoulos, Miller, and Beattie (1992) and Tuokko, Hadjistavropoulos, Miller, Horton, and Beattie (1995) for more information on the scoring manual.

To obtain more detailed information about these and other measures of cognitive function, the interested reader is referred to the 1998 volume by O. Spreen and E. Strauss, *A Compendium of Neuropsychological Tests: Administration, Norms and Commentary*, and the 1995 volume by Muriel Lezak, *Neuropsychological Assessment*.

Alcohol or other substance abuse or misuse can be a source of numerous problems, including the following:

- Behavioral disturbances

- Cognitive problems including delirium

- Affective changes

Brief assessment for alcohol problems is recommended whenever depression is present, as alcohol can be used to self-medicate and problems with it can be more difficult to detect in older adults. Many older adult problem drinkers are widowed or divorced, retired, and not driving as frequently, so the probability of their problem being detected by others is reduced. SAMHSA's Center for Substance Abuse Treatment (CSAT) includes both screening and treatment guidelines in Treatment Improvement Protocol (TIP) #26 (CSAT, 1998, 2006). One screen recommended for use with older adults is the Michigan Alcoholism Screening Test—Geriatric version (MAST-G).

The Michigan Alcoholism Screening Test-Geriatric Version

The MAST-G (Blow, Brower, Schulenberg, Demo-Dananberg, Young, & Beresford, 1992) is a 24-item self-report scale in which each item is responded with a yes or no. It is also available as a 10-item scale called the Short MAST-G (SMAST-G; Blow et al., 1998). Both scales ask about thoughts and behaviors related to possible alcohol abuse such as the following: Is the person embarrassed after social gatherings for drinking too much? When feeling lonely, does having a drink help? Is the person concerned that drinking might be harmful to his health? These "face valid" items seem to encourage honest responses on the part of older adults.

Addressing Misuse of Medication

With older adults, inadvertent misuse of medications is also found. Typically, "street drugs" are not used by the elderly; instead, errors in complying with often complex medication regimens can result in unexpected negative side effects such as cognitive confusion, difficulties concentrating, and changes in mood. In addition, some older adults consciously abuse prescription medications such as painkillers and tranquilizers. These and related issues are discussed in Clifford, Cipher, Roper, Snow, & Molinari (2008). This complex topic is beyond the scope of this manual, but it is mentioned to sensitize the clinician to collecting information carefully and thoroughly as to what medications are being taken on a regular basis and to help the clinician be alert to possible problems in this arena, which then require referral to a medical professional for appropriate treatment.

Assessment of Depression and Anxiety

A thorough review of self-report scales to assess depression or anxiety in older adults can be found in Edelstein et al. (2008; see Tables 2.1 and 2.2). We recommend consideration of three depression scales for use in clinical practice: Beck Depression Inventory II (BDI-II; Beck, Steer, & Brown, 1996), Center for Epidemiologic Studies Depression Scale (CES-D; Radloff, 1977), and Geriatric Depression Scale (GDS; Yesavage et al., 1983). Each has its own pluses and minuses with older adults, as follows.

Beck Depression Inventory II

The BDI-II is the most clinically oriented of this group. Its 21 items include questions on hopelessness and suicide that serve as screening questions for these concerns. There are also a number of somatic items that can complicate the picture, since many somatic symptoms (e.g., fatigue, sleep, and appetite disturbances) can result from medical illnesses in the elderly and not truly be reflective of depression. In addition, the descriptors in 4-point severity scale for each item are sometimes confusing and may need clarification. Often, older adults (even those who are not cognitively impaired) check several answers to the same question, so it is necessary to clarify which response is correct. The BDI-II is copyrighted and can be purchased from the Psychological Corporation in San Antonio, TX.

Center for Epidemiologic Studies Depression Scale

The original 20-item scale contains somatic questions as well as those that reflect psychological distress, but it does not contain any specific question on suicidal thoughts. The response format is based on frequency of occurrence of each symptom: not at all in the past week to most days. This can be confusing for older adults as it requires them to think back over a week's period and give an "average" rating. On the positive side, the CES-D has been translated into multiple languages (e.g., Spanish, Chinese, and Japanese) and so can be used with clients who prefer to respond in their native language. A copy of the full scale can be downloaded free from: www.hepfi.org/nnac/pdf/sample_cesd.pdf. In addition, a copy of the 10-item short scale can be downloaded free from: http://patienteducation.stanford.edu/research/cesd10.pdf.

Geriatric Depression Scale

The GDS was designed specifically for use with older adults. The full scale is 30 items; there are also shorter versions available. Most somatic items have been removed and it employs a simple "yes/no" response format. These features are generally considered advantages in using the scale with older adults as it can be completed even by those with mild cognitive impairment, and the absence of somatic items means the measure taps into the psychological aspects of depression in detail. GDS has been translated into multiple languages and is used around the world. Copies (in English as well as translated versions) and scoring instructions can be downloaded free of charge from http://www.stanford.edu/~yesavage/GDS.html.

Measures of Anxiety

Anxiety frequently co-occurs with depression in older adults; in fact, about half of those with depression report symptoms of anxiety: both physiological (e.g., upset stomach and heart fluttering, which are identified as signs of tension and as not due to medical causes) and psychological (e.g., worry, fear, and mental tension). Specific measures of anxiety in older adults that we use are provided next.

Geriatric Anxiety Inventory

This is a brief measure that has strong psychometric properties, few somatic items, and a dichotomous response format (Pachana, Byrne, Siddle, Koloski, Harley, & Arnold, 2006). It is a good overall choice that assesses what traditionally is considered "anxiety" in the psychiatric literature.

Adult Manifest Anxiety Scale—Elderly Version

This is a multidimensional 44-item measure of chronic (trait) anxiety with three clinical subscales: fear of aging, physiological anxiety, and worry/oversensitivity (AMAS-E; Reynolds, Richmond, & Lowe, 2003; described in Lowe & Reynolds, 2006). It is useful for treatment planning.

Assessment of Suicide Ideation/Hopelessness

It is a fact that older adults have higher rates of suicide than other age groups (except adolescents): 14.7/100,000 vs. the national average of 11.01/100,000 (Centers for Disease Control and Prevention, 2006, 2008). Older adults represent 12% of the U.S. population but 16% of deaths by suicide each year, with males over the age of 75 being the group most likely to complete suicide. Therefore, older depressed individuals must be assessed for suicide risk and protective factors. Heisel and Flett

(2008) have reviewed topics including resilience factors among older adults. Since physical illness increases risk for suicide later in life, the reader is referred to work by Fiske, O'Riley, and Widoe (2008), which reviews health conditions that confer risk. This is an excellent reason to include assessment of the client's medical status in your preliminary assessment and to reevaluate it as treatment progresses.

The two scales frequently used in clinical practice with older adults are Scale for Suicide Ideation (Beck et al., 1979) and Geriatric Suicide Ideation Scale (Heisel & Flett, 2006).

Scale for Suicide Ideation (SSI)

This is a very clinically oriented measure that is generally appropriate for use with mental health outpatients and inpatients (though it is not specific to older adults). It is meant to be an interview guide (not a self-report) that provides a comprehensive assessment of suicide ideation (including reasons for living as well as reasons for dying). Often in practice, a self-report such as the Hopelessness Scale (Beck & Steer, 1993) will be given first; if the client scores high in hopelessness, then the SSI might be used to further explore the situation in detail. Prior research has shown that the high hopelessness and the pessimism item on the BDI predicted suicide completion over a 10-year follow-up (Beck, Steer, Kovacs, & Garrison, 1985).

Geriatric Suicide Ideation Scale

This 31-item multidimensional self-report measure assesses presence and severity of suicide ideation, death ideation, loss of personal and social worth, and perceived meaning in life. Some items tap resiliency factors as well. It has been used successfully with diverse elders (e.g., Chinese and African Americans) and is viewed as "strong" psychometrically by Edelstein et al. (2008). However, they caution that assessment of suicide risk should be conducted as part of a comprehensive clinical assessment as skill and judgment are needed in order to avoid both false positives and false negatives.

Older adults typically have a number of medical problems that need further consideration in developing a therapy regimen. In fact, the client's psychological distress is often due, in large part, to some aspect of their physical condition and to medications they are required to take. It is extremely useful to become aware of their medical status and the implications this might have for your work with them. It is important to forge an alliance with their primary care physician and consider consults with other medical specialists who might be involved in their care. Often, older clients are followed by a multidisciplinary team comprised of allied health professionals as well as medical specialists, as they may have many problems that contribute to their general clinical condition. In this instance, it is helpful to consult with other professionals in the team, which might include physical and occupational therapists, neuropsychologists, social workers, and nurse specialists.

While there are several self-report measures that ask about current illnesses and medications, we recommend asking the client to describe his health status. (Earlier it was suggested that they be asked to *bring* all of their medications as well as contact information for their PCP to the assessment interview.) If the individual appears to be significantly impaired in his ability to care for himself or take care of everyday activities of daily living, there probably is a designated "caregiver" who provides this care. It is recommended to have that person complete one or more of the scales assessing functional dependence/independence, such as the Instrumental Activities of Daily Living scale (Lawton & Brody, 1969; download free from http://www.acsu.buffalo.edu~drstall/iadl.html), to provide information that is relevant for treatment planning. For example, if the client cannot drive, or is unable to care for himself independently, that limits the kind of activities to consider when doing behavioral activation in therapy later on.

Social Supports and Other Domains

It is extremely important to identify the available support resources in the client's living situation and what kind of environment stressors might exist. Also, you should generally determine what might be key cultural and age-cohort factors that require consideration in your work with the client. These data will help to inform treatment decisions.

It is beyond the scope of this manual to provide detailed information about the various measures that assess social support, coping skills, religious beliefs and practices, health beliefs and practices, personality, and other important features of Figure 1.1. However, we can refer the interested reader to the following sources for specific information:

- Kane, R. A., & Kane, R. L. (1981). *Assessing the elderly: A practical guide to measurement.* Lexington, MA: D.C. Heath & Co.

- American Psychiatric Association (2008). *Handbook of psychiatric measures.* Washington, DC: American Psychiatric Publishing Inc. (includes CD-ROM).

- Agronin, M. E., & Maletta, G. J. (Eds.). (2006). *Principles and practice of geriatric psychiatry.* Philadelphia: Lippincott Williams & Wilkins.

Other Information Valuable to Case Conceptualization

Interviews with family members, friends, and other possible informants are highly recommended if the client grants permission. Obtaining others' evaluations of your client's strengths and weaknesses and general behavioral characteristics can be extremely helpful in your therapy work. If assessments have been completed elsewhere, it will be helpful and save time to review and become familiar with as much information as possible before your first session with the client.

Summary and Recommendations

During the initial assessment interview, it is critical to obtain information about a broad range of factors that might be influencing the client's state of mind and mood. Taking a comprehensive approach to assessment will help with treatment planning, and it may serve to highlight issues that were not noted in the original referral or initial contact with the client. A combination of self-report measures and interview-based questions generally yields better results than either one alone. Obtaining input from the client's PCP and his family members, to round out the presentation given by the client alone, is strongly recommended.

Taken together, this information should enable you to decide if this is a suitable client for CBT, that is, someone likely to benefit, given the profile of people who have benefited from previous research studies. This is a "checklist" that we use in our practice to help us decide on the "next steps" in the process:

✓ Can the client adequately process information?

✓ Is he physically well enough to commit to, and attend, sessions on a regular basis?

✓ Are there family conflicts and strains likely to interfere with the client's participation in treatment (e.g., are there lots of "family crises" that the client feels he must attend to?)

✓ What other problems have you detected in addition to depression?

✓ Is concurrent treatment (e.g., pharmacotherapy) indicated? Are referrals to other professionals needed *before* CBT can commence? (e.g., does the client have medical problems such as diabetes that he reports to be poorly managed? If so, referring him back to his PCP to get the diabetes under better control may be indicated, depending on the severity of the condition. Or, if the client has recently lost a spouse, consider referral to a "grief group" along with CBT.)

✓ Are the intensity, and severity, of the depression manageable on an outpatient basis? Most importantly, is the client expressing strong suicidal ideation, or wishes, and/or a definite plan that appears imminent, such that immediate hospitalization is needed?

Assuming the decision (by both parties) is to "move forward," one would end the session by setting up the first CBT appointment. Writing it down for the client, along with giving your card, can help to facilitate memory and compliance.

Chapter 3 | *Age-Related Issues That Affect CBT*

Specific client groups often require specific procedural changes to ensure that the CBT model is applied optimally to facilitate improvement in the client's level of adjustment and quality of life. This is particularly the case for older individuals, who, as we have discussed in Chapters 1 and 2, often undergo numerous social, psychological, and physical health changes that are less evident in quantity and quality in other client groups seeking therapy. This chapter addresses age-related issues that the therapist should keep in mind when using CBT with older clients.

Age Differences in Sensory and Cognitive Function

The changes that occur in cognitive functioning during the late-adult years are well documented. Comprehensive reviews covering many facets of sensory, psychomotor, and cognitive processes can be found in the *Handbook of the Psychology of Aging* (Birren & Schaie, 2005; 6th edition). Detailed descriptions of physical changes that affect behavior in later life are reported by Spirduso and colleagues (Spirduso, Francis, & MacRae 2005), and an overview of this topic can be found in Woods (2008). Finally, we have included a recent reference covering the essentials pertaining to clinical geriatrics (Kane, Ouslander, Abrass, & Resnick, 2008). These authors have provided a brief, reader friendly discussion of common health problems experienced by the elderly and their implications for acute and chronic functioning. For our purposes, it will be useful to review briefly some of the more general patterns of change.

Increasing Variability of Cognitive Processing With Age

Variability in all types of processing, ranging from sensory input to high-level abstract thinking, increases with increasing age. Some individuals in their late 50s and early 60s are already showing signs of mild cognitive impairment (MCI) or even early degenerative dementia, while others in their late 80s or early 90s are still pretty effective in processing new information. Older clients may also evidence substantial variability within themselves. For example, one person may do extremely well on complex cognitive tasks, such as verbal abstract reasoning, but at the same time perform poorly on tasks requiring complex perceptual/spatial reasoning. Another person might perform exceptionally well on spatial reasoning problems, but have very limited verbal and spatial memory. When working with individuals who show such discrepancies, the therapist may have to introduce modifications in the therapy procedures that will minimize the effects of their specific cognitive impairments and maximize the use of their cognitive strengths to help them develop effective coping skills. Thus, as noted in Chapter 2, a cognitive assessment that provides a brief estimate of the client's strengths and weaknesses across a wide array of cognitive abilities can be helpful.

Trends in Functioning Among Older Adults

Despite this increased variability (both across persons and within the same person), there are several consistent trends in cognitive and behavioral functioning across nearly all individuals in the middle- and late-adult years that require special attention by therapists.

Slowed Motor Response

Slowing of motor response speed is perhaps one of the earliest and most profound changes observed, starting in young adulthood and continuing through the remainder of the life span. Changes within the young adult range are minimal and seldom noticed, except in professional athletes. As individuals move into their mid- to late 60s, slowing of responses is notable in many different daily tasks and adaptations are often required to maintain effective performance levels.

Decline in Sensory Functioning

Older individuals often complain of decreased visual acuity. Increased time may also be required to scan and attend to visual details that are important for accurate appraisal of real-life situations. Most older individuals become acutely aware of this problem and adapt by becoming extremely cautious and sometimes indecisive in situations requiring rapid responses.

Increased problems in hearing verbal material correctly is extremely common in the later years. Studies indicate that both high and low frequencies are more difficult to detect, which can distort the specific phonemes characterizing some spoken words. There also appears to be an attentional component that contributes to the older person's difficulty in understanding complex verbal material. Often, older individuals ask others to repeat statements in order to understand what is being said, particularly in situations where there is a high level of background noise, as in unstructured social gatherings.

This can foster tension in interpersonal encounters if it becomes necessary to repeat everything. If this occurs, the older person will often refrain from asking for clarification of verbal comments because of embarrassment. Without adequate comprehension of what is being said, they may fall silent, change the subject, or make an inappropriate response. This pattern may become so habitual that older individuals simply are often unable to follow the theme of a conversation and appear to others as if they are cognitively impaired.

Therapists must watch for this in their work with older clients and adjust their interaction style to be certain that the client comprehends the material being discussed in session. For example, frequently asking the client to summarize what has been discussed can help the therapist judge whether or not there are hearing and/or comprehension problems that will need to be addressed.

Changes in other sensory modalities are not as critical for cognitive processing, per se, but nevertheless are important for the client's general welfare. Decreased ability to taste and smell can change the client's food preferences, which may result in inadequate nutrition and a clear loss of pleasure obtained from eating. Changes in sensory input from the joint and muscle feedback systems and from the vestibular system can influence the older person's ability to adjust posture and maintain optimal balance following rapid movements. Compensatory adjustments in the type and speed of ambulatory movements are often required. Changes of this nature could lead to a decreased quality of life and increased emotional distress if adequate coping strategies are not in place.

Retained Cognitive Abilities Including Social Reasoning

Not all cognitive abilities decline during the late-adult years. Those that rely heavily on highly over-learned information and that don't require rapid decision making or complex motor responses show little change and in fact often increase over time—such as social skills and general fund of information. On the other hand, the ability to comprehend and use complex abstract information, either verbal or spatial in nature, decreases in the later years (as noted earlier) and this change is accentuated if complex rapid responding is required.

This general pattern has implications when working with an older adult in psychotherapy. As many of us do in social situations, a therapist may often judge a client's ability to understand and deal with complex cognitive material based on her social reasoning capability as evidenced in how the client interacts with the therapist. As many social skills either hold up or increase across time, the therapist may *over*estimate the client's ability to understand and deal with more abstract materials. In such cases, the therapist may set the level of difficulty for materials presented in session and out-of-session practice too high, resulting in poor performance and increased stress on the part of the client.

Changes in Learning and Memory

Spontaneous recall of recently learned material tends to decline, although cued recall and to a greater degree recognition memory show less change with time. Furthermore, problems in learning and memory are frequently accentuated in individuals who are experiencing psychological distress. Using *cues* and *recognition* to improve the client's memory function, rather than relying on spontaneous recall, will often facilitate her progress in learning new therapy skills.

Problems with memory function are usually a matter of great concern to older persons. Nearly every time they experience a failure in memory, the common unhelpful thought is that there is "something wrong with my brain." This thought tends to increase anxiety, which in turn makes it difficult to concentrate on specific tasks, which in turn makes efficient learning and remembering even more problematic. Faced with this situation, it is not uncommon for older individuals to have a momentary "catastrophic reaction," thinking that they must be developing dementia, when in fact they are experiencing memory loss that is common and part of normal aging. It is easy to see how this might cause serious distress for some, particularly for those who obtain great satisfaction from their intellectual capabilities. As with many areas where one might be experiencing problems, there is a tendency to focus obsessively on any memory lapse in support of the notion that one's brain is deteriorating in some way, and no amount of solace seems to allay the concerns. It is unfortunate that one of the first memory problems older persons encounter is the inability to remember names of individuals, and this seems to occur with great regularity. Although treated lightly when first noticed in the 40- to 60- year age range, it eventually becomes a primary complaint for many elderly individuals.

If memory problems appear to be a serious issue with a given client, then it is often useful to focus on her memory function very early in the therapy. If the problem is severe, then a thorough neuropsychological assessment is recommended, so that the nature of the problem can be determined. At the same time, this will require modifications in therapy procedures to accommodate the impairment. If the problem is more one of perception and can be remedied, then evidence of improvement will lessen the distress over the memory issue—at least temporarily—and enable work to proceed on other important therapy goals. The therapist should provide up-to-date information highlighting the role of psychological factors in memory problems, such as the negative effect of anxiety and depression on focused attention, accompanied by a few tips on how to improve memory function. These are readily available online from sources such as the Alzheimer's Association (www.alz.org), which offers a good deal of free, downloadable information about enhancing and improving memory function in normal older adults. Seeing improvement in one's memory can often allay some of the catastrophic concerns about degenerative brain disease, particularly if the client tries a few simple procedures that demonstrate positive effects. Although they may not continue to practice the tips they were given, they nevertheless are less likely to believe that they have "brain disease" and in turn experience less distress. This paves the way for focus on other primary complaints and treatment goals that may in fact be large contributors to the client's initial memory disturbance.

Some Myths About Aging and Their Implications for CBT

Rowe and Kahn's 1998 book *Successful Aging* (New York: Pantheon) presented several common negative views of aging, two of which are relevant to this context. First, "to be old is to be sick"; second, and VERY relevant for CBT, is "you can't teach an old dog new tricks." Others—such as older people are too dependent and disengaged, and they are "over the hill" so why bother with psychotherapy of any kind—may come into play as well.

"To Be Old Is to Be Sick"

First, not all older individuals are "sick" or functionally disabled and impaired in their daily lives—at least not totally. A decline in functioning tends to be viewed by clients and family members in "all or none" terms, but older individuals can usually still perform many of their former tasks in modified form.

Although chronic illness is common in adults over the age of 65, in and of itself, it is not synonymous with functional impairment. Also, despite the high prevalence of conditions such as arthritis, hyptertension, heart disease, diabetes, and cancer, older adults do not necessarily consider themselves to be in "poor health." Older people tend to think of their health more in terms of how these different conditions affect their ability to handle everyday life (rather than focusing on the diagnoses themselves). By age 80, about 28% report having some problem with activities of daily diving (ADLs), and 40% report having problems completing instrumental activities of daily living (IADLs). The constraints resulting from these limitations are generally more likely to curtail other activities, which make them feel old (Haber, 2007). Fear of falling is the most common fear reported by older people and is a good example of the interactions among physical health, behavior, and emotional problems: Fear of falling limits activities; clients tend to lose confidence in their ability to avoid falls and to manage well in everyday life, and consequently reduce their activities and thereby reinforce depressive tendencies.

Other physical changes, such as a higher percentage of body fat, less lean muscle mass, and reduction in the vital lung capacity all occur with regularity. Such changes can often reduce their "quality of life" as they cannot, or do not, do activities they used to enjoy. Decreased activity, however, may be due to a sedentary lifestyle. About 40% of older adults are not active at all and inactivity increases with age, so that by age 75, roughly 1 in 3 men and 1 in 2 women engage in no physical activity (Knopf, 2004).

By encouraging clients to learn what their physical limitations actually are, and what they may still be very capable of doing (with appropriate training and support), the negative impact of physical health problems can be reduced, and the individual can be encouraged to have a more active and fulfilling life. Recent studies have shown that moderate exercise decreases depressive symptoms and the likelihood of relapse following gains (Knopf, 2004). As health problems are so common, it is important for the CBT therapist to take the time to learn about the particular conditions the client is experiencing, and most important, how these are affecting her quality of life. Consultation with medical professionals can help the therapist understand possible areas for improvement in everyday function that could be addressed as part of the therapy.

"You Can't Teach an Old Dog New Tricks"

YES you can! Overwhelming evidence has proven this to be the case (cf. Birren & Schaie, 2005). Your firm conviction of this fact will help you be more effective as a therapist in working with the elderly. Older adults themselves may feel that they can't change; it's your job to help them see that they can, and will, if they engage in the program with you. Remember, the evidence is there to support this position.

Often these perceptions of inability to change or learn are based on age-related changes in cognitive processing, as well as changes in sensory-motor function, and limitations due to very real medical conditions. In this case, it is easy to become discouraged and look at the glass as "half empty" rather than "half full." You will need to elicit that belief from the client and family (if it's there), then work with it and counteract it, so that the therapy can proceed. We recommend emphasizing that CBT involves learning new things and then asking the client: When is the last time you learned something new? What was it (probe for examples, however small)? Do you think you are able to learn anything *else* new? Or if the person can't come up with *any* recent new learning, ask: Do you think you will be able to learn something new at this point in time? Very depressed older clients often say "no," that they are not capable of learning, and if so, it is advisable early on in therapy to set up an "experiment" to determine if this is true. Typically, it is not, and you are able to point that out to the client based on empirical evidence.

Many elderly clients, regardless of depression level, will accept this myth as true, but if you challenge how much they *really* believe this adage applies to them, you will find that they often will admit that it doesn't. Nevertheless, the unchallenged acceptance of this belief may set up an expectation of poor learning ability that leads to avoidance of activities requiring them to learn new skills. Avoidance of activities because of a presumed limitation in ability falsely reinforces its validity and can lead to a further reduction in activities and lower self-esteem, which increases the likelihood of depressive symptoms. Thus, challenges that disprove such myths can be extremely beneficial for the client.

A related aspect is the family's role in maintaining, or challenging, this kind of belief. Usually, we recommend that family members be included at least in the initial assessments so that the therapist can get a better sense of how supportive, or obstructive, they have been in the past and are likely to be as the therapy proceeds. Supportive family members who encourage the client to think that she can learn new ways to view herself and her situation can be very helpful. They can reinforce home practice assignments, work with you if new challenges emerge, and add to that sense of hope. On the other hand, nonsupportive family members need to be included periodically in therapy sessions (or in extra meetings without the client, if possible) so that they can at least hear from you in general terms about the treatment plan and the likelihood of success. Sometimes, this will modify their views. Other times, they will remain nonsupportive, in which case treatment goals may need to be modified to better fit the situation.

Why Bother Doing Psychotherapy When "Over the Hill"?

Another common myth that some clients (and psychotherapists) may have is this: Older people are "over the hill" so why bother doing psychotherapy with them? They won't be around much longer anyway. Recent data, however, indicate that people who reach the age of 65 can expect on average to live another 18 years (U.S. Census Bureau, 2001). In our experiences, pointing out that older individuals can still *do* many of the things they did earlier in life (albeit with some modifications possibly in frequency and/or intensity) and that they can still have meaningful roles (in the family, with friends, as a volunteer and possibly even still as an employee) helps them to modify their perspective. There can be a lot of years ahead, and those years can be made more positive by doing a "course" of CBT to learn skills for preventing and/or reducing depression. Doing so *now* can greatly improve overall *quality of life* in the client's remaining years.

Age-related changes often require some modifications in CBT when working with the elderly, particularly those above 75 or 80 years of age.

Therapist Note

■ *We are not talking about major modifications to the practice of CBT. As always, there are certain key elements to be found in every session, such as agenda setting, review of past home practice, using collaborative empiricism to strengthen the therapeutic relationship, focusing on key topics for discussion, using "tools" to teach important points, and assigning new home practice. What's different is HOW these things are done.* ■

Socializing the Older Adult Into Treatment

One of the first major hurdles is getting the older client engaged in the therapy. We will focus on this later as we discuss the content of the early phase of therapy. In this section, we will cover several issues that commonly occur throughout therapy.

Agenda Setting and "Staying on Track"
Problem

Staying on track can be very difficult to do with older adults who need to "tell their story" at length. Often, this leads to wandering "off track" when talking and taking up valuable therapy time with details that are not really that important or relevant to the task at hand.

Main Remedy

You will need to learn the art of gently redirecting the conversation. Many therapists, who are often one to three generations *younger* than these clients, find it difficult to interrupt the elder who is speaking. Begin in the first treatment session (once assessment is complete) to structure the time, and evaluate how much of a problem the tendency to go off on tangents, and not return to the main point, is likely to be for your client. By the second or third time you have noticed this, you will want to discuss the following points:

- Therapy time is very valuable and quite short, given that it is 1 hour once/week (or less frequent, perhaps) and so it is necessary to use the time well.

- To use the time well, you (the therapist) will have to interrupt the conversation at times and redirect it back to the topic at hand.

- To interrupt effectively, it is a good idea to have a signal of some kind that you both know what it means, such as raising a finger or using the "time-out" sign (crossed "t" with both hands).

- You want to interrupt in a respectful way, and, it is important that you both agree on this course of action. (Essentially, you are asking permission to interrupt, which will make you more comfortable doing it as the need arises.)

Other Remedies

Placing time estimates next to each agenda item is also helpful. Since you will have the agenda up on a whiteboard or on a flipchart or at least on a piece of paper, it will be easy to point out to the client that there is only so much time in therapy when she gets off topic.

A related issue is that quite possibly, the client DOES have a lot to share with you: perhaps several important things happened since the last meeting. You can then take the opportunity to rearrange the agenda and add the items that seem important. Asking the client to prioritize them is helpful, since it's unlikely that all can be covered in the time available.

Finally, we have encouraged very talkative clients and/or clients who really do have a lot going on in their lives to keep a journal or diary of these events, which they bring in and share with you. It's best to make a copy of the material so you can read it when there is time to think about how to incorporate this into therapy if it is valuable information.

We have found that by encouraging clients to keep a diary, a good deal of the "pressure" that some feel to tell you everything that's on their minds is reduced, and at the same time, you are conveying respect for their desire to communicate in more detail than the "50-minute hour" permits.

Pacing of How Rapidly New Material Is Presented
Problem

Mild cognitive impairments (e.g., in memory, see earlier discussion) are common, and if material is presented at the same pace as if the client were in their 20s or 30s, there is likely to be confusion and misunderstanding. However, in the typical course of CBT, there is a lot of material to cover, many skills to teach, and not that many sessions to work with.

Remedies

Slowing the Pace: In general, it is recommended to start out by slowing the pace in which material is presented in session. You can begin by talking more slowly than is typical, check that what you are saying is being heard clearly (as discussed earlier), and check for comprehension by asking the client to give frequent summaries of what she is learning throughout the session. In this way, you can "check" for how much is really being absorbed and adjust accordingly. Do not be discouraged if the pace is slower than you would like; it is better for some key material to be processed well than for a lot of material to be processed poorly.

Present Material Multimodally: Say it, show it, and do it. Often, this involves having the client purchase a notebook (and the workbook that accompanies this guide) so that she can write down key points from each session. By keeping the information all together, memory is enhanced and there is less chance of it being misplaced. In addition, it is common to tape-record sessions and give the tape to the client to review. This helps with memory problems for details; also, important points that may have been covered but were forgotten by the client will be remembered when she hears the tape. This kind of multimodal involvement reinforces learning.

Use Memory Aids: Use of memory aids is strongly encouraged. As noted previously, writing down points from session (along with home practice assignments, which will be forgotten very quickly if they are NOT written down, and date and time of next scheduled appointment) encourages the client to review the material between sessions. This enhances memory. In addition, calling the client (brief reminder calls, 5–10 min duration) between sessions to discuss home practice assignments can greatly increase home practice compliance. Clients frequently say that they "forgot to do their home practice," and with older adults that may be very accurate. Finally, written reminders such as Post-it® notes that are done in session and given to the client to place in obvious spots can be helpful.

Developing and Maintaining a Therapeutic Alliance
Problem

The client is typically at least one generation (often 2 or 3) older than the therapist. What else can the therapist do (besides the norm) to enhance the working relationship?

Remedies

- Clarify how the client wishes to be addressed, and how she wishes to address you, and remember to do that from session to session, on the phone, and so on—even if it is not initially that comfortable for you.

- Remember important details of the individual's life history (keep specific notes; know the names of her children and grandchildren; pay attention!)

- Learn to be nondefensive when the client asks about personal details of your life (which almost all do): How old are you? Are you married? Do you have children? grandchildren? Have you worked with many older adults? We recommend that you have answers "ready" to give that you are comfortable with. Dodging the issue by refusing to give any personal information makes the client suspicious of you and seems to damage the therapeutic relationship. Of course, you should disclose the minimum that seems to satisfy the client and that you are comfortable with.

- Be open to feedback and be willing to gently confront "unpleasantness" in the therapeutic relationship. For example, if the client typically cancels therapy appointments with 1 day or less notice, discuss with her how this means you cannot use the time for another client who may need it. On the other hand, if the client brings up something negative about you or the therapy (e.g., "I'm not sure you really understand me; how could you, you haven't been married 50 years" or "you don't have to watch your adult children bringing up your grandchildren with no respect for society"), it is important not to be defensive about your younger age or lack of certain life experiences. You can underscore that you have special training in the problems of later life, and believe that your knowledge and skills will be helpful to the person. Often, it is helpful to point out that you both can learn from each other.

- Acknowledge that therapy can be difficult and requires hard work and commitment; indicate that you too, for example, do "home practice" between sessions in order to make the best use of the time together.

- Give clients credit for specific accomplishments, but avoid generic compliments. For example, "Mary, you did a great job on the thought record this week. I can see that you are learning how to use it effectively. Good for you." It seems that most older people don't get much praise for what they do anymore and a little goes a long way!

Dealing With Countertransference
Problem

The therapist senses that he or she is developing a bit of a "negative attitude" toward a client and begins to hope the client starts canceling appointments, and so on. Therapist may think: "I don't feel I am helping him; he is so slow to change; he is very difficult to work with."

Remedies

As with clients of any age, consult with a colleague if these negative feelings are strong. We recommend that if that does not seem necessary, then begin to deal with your own dysfunctional cognitions. Avoid stereotyping the older adult as "resistant"—instead think about how you could present CBT differently and/or renegotiate therapy goals.

- Use your own feelings as a chance to refocus on what this particular client is doing to create them.

- Remain optimistic about the client's ability to learn and to improve her mood management skills. It just takes longer and requires more work.

- Maintain a problem-solving attitude.

Working as Part of a Multidisciplinary Team
Problem

Most therapists in private practice settings tend to operate "solo" and tend not to make contact with other professionals who are also treating the client as it is generally not necessary. With older clients, however, it may be important to see oneself as part of a "multidisciplinary team" that is working together for the welfare of the client.

Remedies

With older adults, given their medical complexities, it is recommended that written permission be obtained to communicate with the primary care physician, at least, to understand the medical problems and their functional limitations (as discussed earlier). If there is a social worker or case manager involved, this person is also good to get to know as he or she is coordinating other aspects of the client's life that can have an impact on the therapy.

Developing collegial relationships with other providers in the area who serve older adults is also helpful, so that referrals can be made more readily, if necessary, when the course of CBT is over. For example, you should know about senior centers in the region: where they are and how to contact them. They can be an excellent resource for increasing pleasant activities. It's surprising how few seniors know about the centers in their area and have ever actually visited one. It is helpful to become knowledgeable about self-help groups in the area that deal with common problems of later life, such as a sleep disturbance support group or a support group for people living with chronic illness. Expecting the *client* to seek out this kind of information is unrealistic. Most older adults are not "computer savvy" and even so, if they find the information, they are not likely to act upon it. It generally saves time and frustration for the therapist to make the initial contact, obtain the basic information, make the referral, and so on to "lay the groundwork" before passing it along to the client. Suggested national resources to help you get started are included in the appendix.

Other Issues to Consider

Other issues to consider when doing CBT with older adults include the following:

- Sustained low energy level in the client, due to health problems. This may just be a "fact of life" that you need to adapt to. It does not mean the client can't benefit from CBT, but there may need to be a greater emphasis on working cognitively and/or on selecting a very limited range of behaviors to increase.

- Unfamiliarity with concepts and methods of therapy. Most older adults (now in their late 60s, 70s, and greater) grew up in an era when mental illness was frequently treated by inpatient hospitalization. "Talking therapy" was only for the rich or for those who had sufficient time and money to indulge themselves in "just talking" about things. The concept of therapy being a form of treatment that can remove obstacles, improve quality of life, and reduce depression and anxiety is not a common belief among many older adults.

- Control issues with the reactive client: Older adults who have strong issues with "who's in control" can have difficulty with the prescriptive nature of CBT. This is true, of course, at any age but it seems particularly difficult to deal with in an older individual who always has to be "right." Such clients "react" often to following an agenda (even if they participated in creating it), often refuse to do home practice or do something that is quite "their own style," which may or may not be in alignment with the current focus, and may tax the therapist's patience with their incessant need to "word-smith" so that things are discussed, or written down, precisely as the client wants. We have found that the only way to engage this client in CBT is to share the control of the session and the home practice, giving them the lion's share. Use of paradoxical interventions can, at times, also be helpful.

Successful Home Practice With Older Adults

Home practice is an important component of CBT for the elderly. A number of strategies that we have used are discussed here. We have also included a reference list of others who have emphasized the critical nature of home practice to successful therapy outcome. Therapists are encouraged to use their own creativity to help tailor home practice to meet the needs of our diverse aging population and to employ a variety of their own strategies to address challenges to home practice.

Checkpoints for Success Specific to the Elderly

Successful home practice rests on a number of "checkpoints for success." Note that many critical points that are common for individuals at all ages have not been covered. This section focuses on specific strategies to use with older adults.

Checkpoint 1: Recognizing Beliefs About "Home Practice"

✓ Home practice suffers when ageist assumptions and therapist pessimism lead to poorly articulated assignments. The following are some common therapist beliefs: *I feel I am being disrespectful when I assign home practice to older clients; She has done it this way for over 60 years, so how can I expect her to change? Consistent assignments aren't as important as my relationship with Mrs. Roberts, are they?* Therapists may need to ask themselves: *What evidence exists that the client cannot complete home practice appropriately tailored to meet her needs? What evidence is there that the client cannot collaborate in developing home practice, taking into account her situation (including the sociocultural context in which she lives)?*

✓ Older clients also have views about home practice, and therapists need to be sensitive about this from the outset. The term "homework" itself can hold unpleasant connotations or may be considered demeaning, especially for people with limited schooling or who did poorly in school or completed little formal education. Collaborate to find more palatable terms for homework using the clients' own language and experience. For example, substitute phrases for the *process* of homework such as "home practice," "handling their job," "testing experiments," or "learning new habits," and refer to homework *assignments* as "experiments," "practice sheets," "journal writing," or "mind push-ups."

Checkpoint 2: Appreciating Diversity and Tailoring Home Practice for Individual Differences

✓ Diversity actually increases rather than decreases with age when we consider the wide range of personal histories and individual sociocultural contexts of older clients. Seek out ways to acknowledge these histories and contexts to foster collaborative development of suitable assignments and to maximize out-of-session practice.

✓ Demonstrating respect for older clients and their personal stories can serve as the cornerstone of creative and successful home practice. For example, (a) encourage clients to share their personal stories using their own descriptors for distress, problem definition, and treatment strategies, including home practice; (b) gain a clear understanding of the important role significant others (e.g., family, community leaders, and cultural institutions) hold for the client with regard to problem definition, treatment, and home practice; and, (c) increase your understanding of and respect for the use of religion and other spiritual practices in tandem with CBT.

✓ Do not make automatic assumptions about what will or will not work as home practice. Take it slowly: gather the necessary information from the older client (and other reliable sources as needed); consistently check in about home practice assignments along the way; and be mindful to work within the client's sociocultural context. Two recent books that focus on ethnic diversity in sociocultural processes and CBT are:

- Gallagher-Thompson, D., Steffen A., & Thompson, L. W. (Eds.). (2008). *Behavioral and cognitive therapies with older adults.* New York: Springer.
- Hays, P. A., & Iwamasa, G. Y. (Eds.). (2006). *Culturally responsive cognitive-behavioral therapy: Assessment, practice, and supervision.* Washington, DC: American Psychological Association.

Checkpoint 3: Recognize Late-Life Physical Challenges

✓ Successful home practice completion with physically ill, disabled, or frail clients often requires the therapist to develop new approaches, including: (a) increased knowledge of common illnesses and functional impairments; (b) more frequent contact with various health care providers; (c) greater flexibility in treatment appointment times and locations (e.g., nursing homes, hospitals, clinics, and family residences); (d) more emphasis on teamwork with the older client's support systems; and (e) an even closer collaboration with clients in the development of assignments.

✓ Consider securing permission to contact formal and informal support network members to help facilitate home practice compliance, such as helping with writing tasks, setting up audiovisual equipment, or joining pleasant activities. However, avoid the development of coercive systems or tactics to promote home practice compliance, and take the appropriate steps to protect confidentiality and respect privacy.

✓ Work with clients and their support systems to resolve practical barriers to home practice completion (e.g., for the hearing impaired, use in session amplifiers, tape sessions to take home if they have equipment to amplify audiotapes, or identify relevant bibliotherapy material).

✓ Adjust the goals and pace of therapy, including relevant home practice; begin with modest steps to support success, and recalibrate the pace to fit client progress. Break assignments into several steps or components and celebrate accomplishments. Design assignments that minimize fatigue and discomfort.

✓ Finally, remain mindful of "excess disability" (i.e., whether or not additional amounts of disability beyond that imposed by the disease or physical impairment are being experienced as a result of the clients' emotional distress). Educate clients and their support systems that depression is a reversible problem that can be distinguished from the older adult's physical challenges. Moreover, work collaboratively to challenge all-encompassing labels of the self as only a "burden."

Checkpoint 4: Describe, Demonstrate, Do, and Discuss (The 4 "Ds")

✓ These four steps help clients develop new skills and transfer established skills to more challenging situations. Client and therapist role-plays of stressful situations in the client's life are an example of a strategy that easily incorporates the 4 Ds; here, the dyad describes and discusses the situation, thoughts, and behaviors, demonstrates and practices client responses to the situation, and then discusses in detail what has transpired in this exercise, which segues nicely into a negotiation of an out-of-session practice to do the work.

✓ An array of assignments and practice strategies can incorporate the 4 Ds, including behaviorally based experiments such as relaxation exercises (module 5) or pleasant event schedules (module 3) to written exercises like journaling and Unhelpful Thought Diaries (UTDs) (module 4).

✓ Particularly for the elderly, it is important to spend time elaborating on the home practice to be accomplished. This is illustrated by the 4 Ds. Doing a sample assignment in session is especially helpful in increasing compliance.

Checkpoint 5: Modify Home Practice for Clients With Mild to Moderate Cognitive Impairment

✓ Several modifications can be used to enhance home practice for older adults with MCI (e.g., audiotape or videotape sessions for home review; develop structured and simple activity schedules for routine use).

✓ Simplify and reduce the number of concepts used, and then reuse and reliably reinforce them. For example, for some mildly impaired clients, the UTD can be effectively reduced to three columns of "Thought", "Feeling," and "New Thought" or "Thought," "New Thought," and "New Feeling."

✓ Design and use a simple notebook or calendar to schedule sessions and hold intervention and home practice material. Identify the best and remove the rest of the material in the notebook. Brainstorm with the client (and as appropriate a family member of the client) to pick one place at home to consistently keep the notebook or calendar.

Checkpoint 6: Overcoming Common Barriers to Home Practice Assignments

When older clients fail to either begin or finish home practice assignments, talk with them about this directly, and work together to find strategies to enhance completion. However, if the problem persists, conduct a more thorough evaluation. In any case, home practice incompletion is typically useful fodder for therapy and often reflects some aspect of the client's target complaints or therapeutic goals. Again, a process of Socratic questioning can be particularly useful in addressing home practice problems.

Early Phase of Therapy

Overview

A number of tasks must be accomplished during the first few sessions if the therapy is to be successful. They can be grouped into three components: (1) The first involves the completion of the initial clinical assessment, which hopefully was underway before the first therapy session (see Chapter 2). (2) The second focuses on engaging the client in therapy and enhancing the client's motivation for compliance. (3) The final component involves the completion of a case conceptualization, which provides the initial guidelines for the treatment. The case conceptualization is often changed during therapy as more relevant information becomes available. All these tasks usually take 2–3 sessions.

The therapist typically will focus on all three throughout the early phase. The first component is guided by the seven content areas outlined in the model and discussed in Chapters 1 and 2. Activities in the second component can be summarized as the 5 Es for effectiveness:

- EASE the client into a therapy mode. The process of psychotherapy is usually a unique experience for elderly clients, and they must acquire a new way of thinking and behaving as they become familiar with the expectations and procedures involved in CBT.

- ELICIT several target complaints (usually three at the outset), which are then used to develop specific treatment goals. The therapist and the client work together to choose goals that can be attained within a short period of time. Once established, goals should be prioritized so that items placed on the treatment session agenda will have maximal relevance for the client.

- EXPLAIN the CBT model in a straightforward manner to help the client understand and accept the rationale for CBT.

- EMPHASIZE the importance of home practice, since the empirical data clearly show that out-of-session practice facilitates the effectiveness of the therapy.

- ENCOURAGE the client to continue in therapy by developing a strong empathic relationship and engendering a positive attitude about the outcome of therapy.

The third component, formulation of a case conceptualization, continues throughout the first few sessions and is necessary to maximize the effectiveness of treatment. Table I.1 summarizes focal issues at the start of therapy.

Table I.1 Focal Issues at the Start of Therapy

- Resolving mobility and transportation problems
- Discussing client–therapist age discrepancy, sharing personal information, and not apologizing for being 1 or 2 generations younger
- Developing ways to compensate for sensory loss
- Establishing tactful, firm ways to limit rambling, "story telling," and unfocused use of time
- Encouraging hope and positive expectations for improved quality of life
- Developing a therapeutic relationship

Chapter 4

Module 1: Introduction to Cognitive-Behavioral Therapy

(Corresponds to chapter 1 of the workbook)

(1–3 Sessions)

Materials Needed

- Copy of client workbook
- Whiteboard or easel

Outline

- Review client history and determine the "chief complaint" using Beck Depression Inventory-II (BDI II) or other appropriate measure
- Present the CBT approach to the treatment of depression
- Describe the A-B-C model
- Explain the downward spiral of negative changes
- Discuss expectations for cognitive-behavioral therapy
- Discuss the importance of home practice
- Summarize session using checklist
- Give mutual feedback
- Encourage client to use "gift of rewards"
- Confirm next appointment
- Assign home practice
- Begin to formulate case conceptualization (therapist only)

Therapist Note

■ *Note that the material covered here can take 1 or 2 sessions, depending on the client. If the client is bright, motivated for therapy, and not severely depressed, this can be completed in 1 meeting. However, 2 sessions are generally required to cover the information presented here. Little progress will be made in addressing treatment goals until these initial steps have been accomplished. Sometimes, if the client is cognitively impaired or otherwise has low motivation, the early phase may continue into an additional session.* ■

Client History and Complaint Assessment

Before the first session (in waiting room), have the client complete the Beck Depression Inventory-II (BDI-II) or another appropriate self-report measure for depressive symptoms to establish baseline level. Begin the first session by going over the client's history from the file and/or intake interview. Determine what is the "chief complaint" (i.e., what is bringing the person into treatment at this time), and use that information to discuss the possible treatment goals. It is also helpful to elicit other complaints as well. Often, the "chief complaint" is complex and may take considerable time before any improvement is evident. Other complaints can be prioritized, and the therapist and the client can work collaboratively to select one where improvement is likely to be seen in a shorter period of time. Success experiences in dealing with less complex complaints can increase the client's sense of mastery and self-efficacy. With success, motivation and compliance typically remain high. The client can use this success experience as a model for working on other complaints.

Therapy Goals and CBT Model

The translation of "target complaints" into therapy goals should be completed by the end of Session 2 or Session 3 (and is explained more in the next session material). You will be asking about complaints and problems the client has, but we recommend that you don't go into too much detail here. Rather, after showing interest and concern, inform the client that you will come back to these complaints later and set up some specific goals to address them. For example, you might say:

Before we start with your specific reasons for coming in, we want to show you how this therapy works and talk about the details so that you'll have a good understanding of what we're going to be doing.

Pay particular attention to the person's physical health, medications, social support networks, and other factors, as outlined in Figure 1.1 and discussed in Chapter 2. This information will be helpful in prioritizing complaints and developing therapy goals that are realistically attainable.

Dealing With "Story Telling"

When reviewing client history and current situation, most older adults begin to "tell stories" about themselves and often ramble on for quite sometime. They tend to be very concerned that the therapist get the maximum amount of information about their physical condition and possible bases for their problems. It is necessary to gently but firmly bring them back to focus on the agenda and the topic at hand. Over time, older clients learn to curb their desire to "just talk," but initially this can be a struggle.

We recommend that in the very first treatment session you establish some sort of "signal" for interrupting and redirecting the discussion, for example, a raised finger, or making the "time-out" (T) sign with both hands, or touching your watch. You will need to explain *why* you are doing this (because therapy time is precious, is relatively short, and there is a lot to be done) and establish that making the signal is going to be acceptable to them. Contrary to what you might expect, older adults are generally appreciative of your efforts in this regard.

If the person really has a lot to say that *is* relevant to the treatment, rather than use valuable in-session time to hear it all, you can ask them to keep a diary or notebook of these thoughts and experiences and bring it to the sessions. You can then take a few moments to scan the content (e.g., while the client is filling out questionnaires in the waiting room) and if something really critical to the case is present, you can ask about it during the session. Alternatively, you can ask clients to audio record stories/anecdotes/experiences that they think are relevant for your understanding of them and agree to listen to one or two such tapes, again to glean critical information likely to be relevant to treatment. See Chapter 3 for more tips on working with older clients.

Presentation of CBT Approach

Four Components

By now, clients may be asking, "What exactly is this treatment that I am starting?" Before getting to the "nuts and bolts" of how this treatment can help, it will be useful to describe the four important components of the cognitive-behavioral approach and how they interact with one another to explain depression or anxiety. These four components reflect on one's current health status, thoughts, behaviors, and emotions. As this explanation might seem abstract, and it may be difficult for clients to see how it might apply to their problems, use the example of John in the workbook (or a similar one of your preference) to show how the approach works. Diagram the interaction of behaviors, health, thoughts, and mood to demonstrate how they affect each other (see Figure 4.1).

Point out that each connection has an arrowhead in two directions. Although the client will be concentrating on how to change his negative

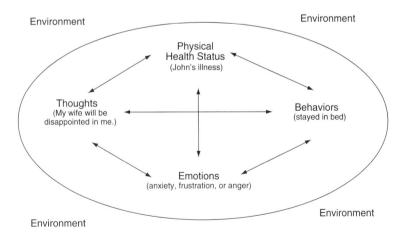

Figure 4.1

Cognitive-Behavioral Model.

emotions, note that the relationships within this model also work for positive emotions.

Also note that we put the word "environment" surrounding the model. Explain that environment refers to the events and the people around the client that affect what he does and thinks, as well as how he feels physically and emotionally. Inform the client that in the course of therapy, he is going to be looking at many different situations in his environment to see how they affect these four components.

We recommend completing a personal example based on the client's situation if there are problems with comprehension or "buy-in." Have the client fill in the blank diagram in the workbook.

How Cognitive-Behavioral Therapy Works

Explain how cognitive-behavioral therapy works as follows:

People usually come to therapy because they do not feel good emotionally for one reason or another. (Circle emotions on the diagram.) *Unfortunately, it is not possible for me to "reach in" and change how you feel. This program also does not try to change your physiology directly through drugs or other means. That leaves us with two factors, thoughts and behavior. CBT can help you change what you think and what you do. You can learn how to change your thinking so that you are not as upset or depressed or nervous about things. You can also make changes to your behavior by learning to build in more pleasant activities into your schedule, express yourself more clearly, and solve problems systematically.*

Emphasize that CBT teaches skills to change thoughts and behaviors and thereby improves mood.

A-B-C Model

Illustrate to the client how CBT can help improve thinking using the A-B-C model. "A-B-C" signifies: Antecedent (or event), Belief, and

Antecedent: What Happened?	Beliefs or Thoughts	Consequences: How Did This Make You Feel?

Figure 4.2
A-B-C Model.

Consequences (emotional). Draw the diagram shown above (figure 4.2) on the whiteboard.

Use the following example to work through the A-B-C model with the client.

> *Assume that you are going up on an elevator when suddenly you receive a sharp poke in the ribs. What goes through your mind?* (The client will usually give a mixture of thoughts and feelings. Try to elicit both, while differentiating the two.)

> *Good! So you think to yourself, "This person is going to rob me,"* (write this under the "Beliefs" column) *and you feel "scared,"* (write this under the "Consequences" column) *or you might think "what an inconsiderate person,"* (write this under the "Beliefs" column) *and feel irritated* (write this under the "Consequences" column). *Now assume that you turn around and you notice the person who poked you is blind. How do you feel now?* (Elicit responses separating "Beliefs" and "Consequences" column information.)

> *What is different in these two situations?* (Try to get the client to explain some variation of "I learned something new about the situation.") *Right! You turned around and gained information that you didn't have before in order to have a more positive reaction.*

> *This is a small example of how CBT works. You will learn various ways to "turn around" your thoughts, assumptions, and perceptions in order to gain new insights and more helpful beliefs that will lead to more positive emotions.*

If there is time, repeat the A-B-C "chain" using an example from the client (vs. this impersonal example). This will facilitate learning.

■ *It is helpful to have a "checkpoint" here and ask the client for a brief summary of key points to check basic understanding of CBT and how it works.* ■

Downward Spiral

Tell the client to keep in mind an important idea in CBT is that these four dimensions—thoughts, feelings, behaviors, and health status—have a notable influence on one another and that this influence is reciprocal in nature. Thus, a negative thought stemming from an unpleasant event can affect behaviors or emotions, which in turn can affect thoughts, and so on. Often, these components can start a downward spiral of negative changes that can throw a person into a tailspin, leading to depression or an anxiety disorder (see Figure 4.3).

This illustration shows that "giving in" to the "slowed down" feeling that often comes with depression leads to a downward spiral (do less → feel worse → do even less, and so on). Clients will learn ways of stopping this tailspin and also reversing it. Point out to the client that the figure on the right shows how a person can "pull out" of a tailspin. The goal of therapy will be to stop a tailspin before it gets started by changing the client's behaviors and thoughts that could lead to a downward spiral. The client will also learn techniques to reverse the tailspin and move himself in an upward spiral.

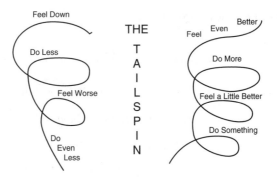

Figure 4.3
Tailspin of Thoughts, Activities, and Emotions.

Discuss expectations for cognitive-behavioral therapy with the client. A common response to the beginning of cognitive-behavioral therapy is, "It sounds good, but can this help me?" Or "This is too simple (or too hard) to solve the problems I have." Assure clients that many research studies have shown that people with serious, complicated problems have found the cognitive-behavioral approach helpful. No matter whether they are "a little blue" or even seriously depressed, or whether they feel a little nervous about something or have extreme panic, this approach might be the thing to help them feel better and function more effectively.

We also work with many older people who begin therapy with the belief that they are "too old to change," or that their beliefs have been around for so long, "it seems hopeless." The research mentioned previously has also included careful studies about whether older people have success in this therapy equivalent to younger adults. Emphasize that it has been discovered that they absolutely do. The client *can* successfully change his thoughts and behaviors as he learns and practices these skills.

It is important to explore your client's past therapy experiences, and clarify how CBT is different from other types of therapy. Explanations of the client role, therapist role, the collaborative relationship, goals for therapy, and home practice are often necessary.

Roles of Client and Therapist

Tell the client that he can expect that his therapist

■ is an expert on the latest techniques in CBT with older adults,

■ is experienced in working with the unique concerns of older people,

■ will work very hard to understand his problems,

■ will help him learn the skills he needs to reach his therapy goals,

- will maintain continuity of work accomplished from session to session,

- will make every effort to reschedule appointments if one is missed or cancelled,

- will expect him to be an active participant and will encourage his collaboration on practice assignments.

Next, explain what is involved in being a client of CBT. The client is expected

- to be open with his therapist about his concerns and any difficulties he is having with the material,

- to arrive on time for sessions and to call if he needs to cancel or reschedule,

- and to be an active member of the relationship, which involves practicing skills in between sessions and being open to discussing the difficulties in completing home practice.

The Collaborative Relationship

The heart and soul of CBT is the formation of a collaborative relationship between the client and the therapist. You begin to develop this by listening to the client and expressing empathy for his situation. It is helpful to discuss past therapy experiences by comparing and contrasting those experiences with CBT. Explain that the collaborative relationship means that *both* the client and the therapist take an active role in understanding the problems that brought the client to therapy, defining goals, and working to achieve goals through the end of therapy.

Goals for Therapy

CBT includes setting goals and working toward them step by step. The outlining of specific goals for therapy makes tracking progress a measurable task. This process will be covered in the second session.

Importance of Home Practice

Emphasize the importance of practicing new skills in between sessions. Practice is one of the best ways we know to make the therapy skills a routine part of daily life. Assignment for home practice should be given at the end of every session. Many clients are not comfortable with the term "homework." So, if need be, substitute a term for it that will enhance compliance from the client.

Many life circumstances make it difficult for clients to complete home practice. For example, time constraints, a difficult assignment, or fears of doing it "wrong" commonly interfere with completing home practice. Some clients may feel resentful of a therapist "telling them what to do," or sometimes clients think that the home practice is silly or useless. Avoiding home practice can seriously interfere with a client's progress, so it is helpful to engage in a dialogue about a home practice task and find strategies to enhance compliance. See Chapter 3 for suggestions for common problems.

Recommended home practice assignments are listed at the end of each chapter.

Summary and Response

Ask the client to summarize his understanding of the CBT and A-B-C models and the program. Be gentle about correcting erroneous ideas and also use this as an opportunity to reinforce what the client did correctly understand. In the workbook, the last page of each chapter contains a checklist/summary of points discussed and skills suggested. The therapist and the client should get into the habit of completing it together at the end of each session. For more insightful clients, you may want to just start it during the session and then assign the rest for home practice.

Mutual Feedback

Allow about 5 min for mutual feedback at the end of this and all subsequent sessions. Model for the client by giving your own feedback as to how you think the session went. Ask the client for both negative and positive feedback. Encourage honesty, and explain that this is important information to help you in adjusting the pacing, tone, and content of future sessions. Some specific suggestions we recommend are:

- "What did you like about today's session?"

- "Were there things I said or did that rubbed you the wrong way or that you thought were off base?"

Gift of Rewards

Explain to the client that committing to actively change certain areas of his life is a major decision. As stated earlier, this is hard work that will require a good deal of attention. Ask the client how he can treat himself well as he works on these difficulties. Strongly encourage the client to think about nice things that he can do for (or say to) himself as celebrations for even small steps of success.

Confirmation of Next Session

End by confirming the date and time of the next session. Older clients often have memory problems and/or multiple medical problems that can interfere with therapy time, so be sure clients check their calendar and write down the date and time of the next session. Give clients your phone number and emphasize the need for 48 hours' advance notice for cancellations.

Home Practice

✎ Have client complete the blank CBT Model Worksheet.

✎ Have client complete the A-B-C chain.

✎ Have client review corresponding workbook section and answer summary questions.

✎ Encourage client to come up with some ideas for rewards.

By the end of the first two or three sessions, the therapist should be able to formulate a working case conceptualization that will guide initial choice of interventions. The case conceptualization could be based on any one of several models that are currently used in the field. One of the most frequently used approaches was developed by Persons, Davidson, and Tomkins (2001; see in particular pages 25–53). Their approach contains the following actions: (1) making a comprehensive problem list—even though treatment is likely to focus on only a few of them—including medical problems, family stress, and so on; (2) highlighting one or two problems from the list for initial focus. For each, you would write out a description in concrete, behavioral terms, based on what you know at this point; (3) noting Axis I diagnoses and diagnoses on other axes, if possible; (4) developing a "working hypothesis" about what is the most important presenting problem or chief complaint that brought the patient into therapy; (5) listing the strengths or assets the patient brings to the situation (e.g., coping skills, prior history, and strong support system); (6) making a tentative treatment plan including possible goals, modalities, and interventions to be used; any adjunctive therapies that seem indicated; and obstacles the therapist can see possibly interfering with therapy.

This case conceptualization serves as a "road map" to help you get started and as a "reference check" periodically as therapy proceeds.

An alternative approach that we prefer to use when working with older adults was developed by Wright and colleagues (Wright, Basco & Thase, 2006). It includes consideration of (1) diagnoses and symptoms; (2) formative influences (from earlier in life); (3) situational issues related to the problem; (4) biological, genetic, and medical factors likely to be impacting the situation; (5) strengths and assets of the patient; (6) an overview of treatment goals; and (7) possible schemas (underlying beliefs) that are maintaining the depression. For a detailed explanation of how to work with this way of conceptualizing CBT for an individual patient, see pages 51–61 in the book by Wright et al. (2006); the book also includes several case examples to work through if you are unfamiliar with this technique. The particular form/worksheet used by this group is on page 266. This and other useful forms from this book can be downloaded free of charge in pdf format from http://www.appi.org/pdf/wright.

To the extent that this information is available by the second or third session, the clinician will want to consider as many of these factors as possible when developing the "working hypothesis" as to what the core issues are, which in turn informs the treatment plan. Consideration of these multiple factors before developing a treatment plan is consistent with our earlier comments in this book about the need to evaluate multiple concomitant issues when working with older adults (see Figure 1.1 in Chapter 1).

We recommend the use of a form to record the case conceptualization and have provided a template in this chapter. In addition, the form can include space for the therapist to record difficult situations and the automatic thoughts, feelings, and behaviors associated with the situation or event, as well as space for recording possible related schemas, so that the clinician can keep on referring to this (and filling it in/revising it/updating it) as more information about the particular client becomes available. We recommend that therapists periodically update their understanding of the case specifics.

Therapist Note

■ *The therapist can develop any type of recording form that is helpful to the clinician in his or her setting. For example, those working in nursing homes or other residential care facilities may want to note more about the environmental influences on thoughts and behaviors than would be typical when working in a outpatient setting.* ■

Case Conceptualization

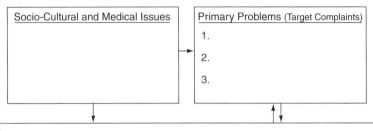

Socio-Cultural and Medical Issues	Primary Problems (Target Complaints)
	1.
	2.
	3.

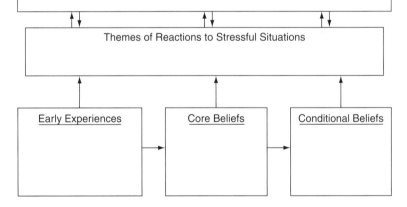

Characteristic Ways of Reacting to Negative Stressful Situations

Cognitive (Recurrent Negative Thoughts):

Behavioral (Compensatory and/or Self-defeating Ways of Responding):

Emotional (Typical Feelings):

Themes of Reactions to Stressful Situations

Early Experiences	Core Beliefs	Conditional Beliefs

After developing the case conceptualization, it is recommended to share it with the client and get feedback as to its accuracy. This takes some of the "mystery" out of therapy. If you can share with the client what you think is causing and/or maintaining his depression and are able to get his "buy-in" in general terms, you are well on your way to developing a strong collaborative relationship. In short, having a "road map" is generally helpful to the client as well as to the therapist. Encouraging the client to share your conceptual view of the situation promotes understanding and helps you both to be "on the same footing." Occasionally, the client will disagree about what to prioritize on the problem list, or what is "driving" the problem, or what the treatment plan should be. This may lead to a useful reworking of the conceptualization, if done collaboratively.

Revising the Case Conceptualization

You should revise the case conceptualization as new information becomes available. Referring back to the case formulation is also helpful if the therapy becomes "stuck." You may have overlooked something that could move the process forward. Finally, reviewing the case conceptualization is also helpful in thinking about the timing of termination.

Chapter 5

Module 2: Identifying Target Complaints and Setting Goals

(Corresponds to chapter 2 of the workbook)

(1–3 Sessions)

Materials Needed

- Copy of client workbook

- Whiteboard or easel

- Target Complaint Worksheet

- Goal Setting Worksheet

Outline

- Review the BDI

- Set the agenda

- Review home practice

- Identify and prioritize target complaints

- "Translate" target complaints into treatment goals

- Discuss how progress is made toward goals

- Summarize session

- Give mutual feedback

- Set schedule

- Assign home practice

Therapist Note

▪ *By now, you most likely have identified several target complaints, and now you are ready to turn them into therapy goals. This may take 1 or at most 2 sessions, depending on the complexity of the client. By the end of the third session, this work should be completed, so that you can select which intervention module to begin with in the next session. In our experience, taking longer to get to this point is discouraging to the client and may lead to premature termination.* ▪

Reviewing the BDI

Before starting the second session, quickly examine the total score on whatever symptom rating form is being used to monitor progress, and note increase or decrease. Most often this will be done using the BDI-II or the short form BDI. For the purpose of continuity, we will refer to that step as "Reviewing the BDI," but choose measurements that are relevant to your client.

Setting the Agenda

It is very important to begin setting an agenda quite early on in treatment so that bad habits of rambling, talking, or unstructured use of time do not get established—it is harder to break them once established than it is to prevent them from occurring. Tell the client that setting an agenda will help you make the best use of the available time.

After the brief check-in, the first item on the agenda should always be home practice review. If this is not done, the client will soon assume that home practice is not that important, despite what you might say, and so compliance will be minimal. A sizable body of research says that depressed clients who do at-home assignments regularly obtain greater benefit from therapy and have less difficulty generalizing what is learned in therapy to the rest of their lives. Also, doing home practice is a skill that the client can use after the therapy is over.

It is wise in the early sessions to take most of the responsibility for setting what you think will be a useful, productive agenda. Besides home practice review, you might add a particular idea that seems pertinent, such as getting more information or history about a certain event or period in the client's life or finding out more about the client's family, living, or job situations. *Always* ask the client to add to the agenda (e.g., "What do you want to talk about today?"). Add to the list and then prioritize. (Also later on, it's good to add time estimates for each item so that the session moves along and everything gets at least some time.)

Home Practice Review

If home practice wasn't done, discuss what the problem might be: lack of clarity of assignment; lack of time on client's part; lack of motivation; no real belief in the model; and so on. You need to elicit reasons and respond within a CBT framework (e.g., "Treat this as an experiment; it would be good for you to collect data about whether or not doing home practice is helpful rather than to just assume it isn't..."). See the home practice section in Chapter 3 for information on how to troubleshoot and suggestions for gaining cooperation.

Identifying and Prioritizing Target Complaints

"Target complaints" refer to the client's description of what situations or symptoms are troublesome. We ask about these so that specific measurable behavioral goals for change can be set. We recommend the identification of two or three target complaints for the course of therapy.

1. Identify the main target complaint.

2. In what situations does this occur?

3. What does the client think is the cause of this difficulty?

4. Has this problem come up before?

5. What strategies have been used in the past to cope with this problem?

6. The client rates the severity of this problem from 1 (least severe) to 10 (most severe).

All six components are explored for each problem. As you discuss, the client should complete the Target Complaint Worksheet, if possible. Use this additional information to help the client prioritize her problems. The workbook includes the case example of Mabel. Use this example (or a similar one of your preference) to explain how to think about target complaints and how to set goals. Also use this example to illustrate how Mabel obtained more details about her first problem to help shape her goals.

Translating Target Complaints into Goals

The difference between a target complaint and a goal is that a goal is a well-defined plan of change (whether focusing on behaviors or beliefs) that is important, time-limited, specific, realistic, positive, and measurable. Each of these properties is defined next (see the workbook for examples for Mabel).

Important

Emphasize that a person's goal must be a priority for her or else she will not have the motivation to work on it.

Time-Limited

Remind the client that CBT is a short-term treatment, therefore, the goals set must be manageable within the time allowed.

Specific

Explain that if a goal is too complicated, or depends on too many components and regulations in order to be met, it is not a good recipe for success. It is always recommended that goals be straightforward and be targeted to a definite area of one's life.

Realistic

Emphasize that a goal must be something that one can achieve independently.

Positive

Often, when people are depressed, they phrase their needs in terms of losses or negatives. Inform the client that stating her goal with positive language will help her begin to understand how she can be in control of the changes that she wants to make.

Measurable

In order for the client to recognize changes in her goals, it is important that the stated goal can be assigned a value along the 10-point scale at the beginning of treatment. The same scale will then be used to rate the status of the complaint at different times throughout therapy. Aside from measuring change, the comparison of these values can initiate the discussion about which strategies have been helpful to making change, or if little change has been seen, what new strategies can be introduced to enhance improvement.

Continue with the case example with an explanation of how a target complaint becomes a specifically stated goal. Use the example of Mabel's Goal Setting Worksheet in the workbook (Figure 2.2) to illustrate the process.

For the remainder of the session, work with the client to complete a blank Goal Setting Worksheet for each of her target complaints. Be sure to ask key questions that may not have occurred to the client. For larger target complaints, help the client break them into smaller separate ones. Also address any limitations of time, money, material, or skills that may interfere with the client's goals. If it is not possible to complete all of this during the session, at least some of the remaining work can be assigned as home practice, to be brought to the next session, where it will be completed by the two of you together.

Therapist Note

■ *Keep in mind that by the conclusion of session 3, or at most session 4, there should be two to three treatment goals established, that were worked on collaboratively by you and the client. They will be used to inform the case conceptualization (see previous material) and to help you monitor progress throughout therapy.* ■

Progress Toward Goals

If there is time in session, explain that progress toward goals is not linear; rather there are "ups and downs" with the overall progress showing improvement. This is a useful concept since many clients think that getting to the goal isn't going to be too hard, now that it is clearly identified. It is good to correct this misconception early on, to reduce the experience of disappointment and disillusionment. If there is not time in this session, be sure to cover this point at the next session.

Explain how progress is made gradually (i.e., successive approximation). Clients often expect change to happen immediately once the process of therapy begins. Illustrate this expectation with Figure 5.1.

It is important to discuss the process of change and help the client to avoid thinking in extremes. Help clients to avoid thinking that if goals are not reached quickly, then "nothing" was accomplished. In addition, emphasize that progress on set goals rarely occurs at a steady pace, or in a continuous direction, like climbing steps. Illustrate with Figure 5.2.

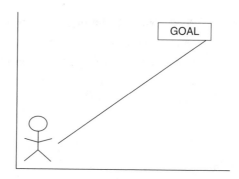

Figure 5.1

Client Expectation of Progress.

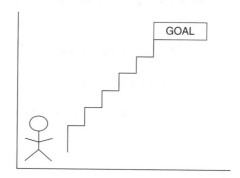

Figure 5.2

Steady Progress.

Figure 5.3

Usual Progress.

Explain to the client that it is difficult to learn a new way of thinking and new behaviors that have seldom or never been tried out before. Furthermore, making the effort and showing progress is easier some days than others. Most change happens with setbacks in between and looks more like a "sawtoothed" curve. Illustrate with Figure 5.3.

When reviewing the progress of goals, make sure clients evaluate the overall process, not just compare the result of one week against the result of the previous week. Just as importantly, encourage clients to recognize and then reward themselves for each step made toward achieving the goal.

Summary of Session

The importance of summaries was discussed in the previous chapter. Help the client answer the following questions on the summary sheet in the workbook:

- What were the key points brought up in this session?

- What skills did I learn?

- What assignments might help me practice these skills?

Mutual Feedback

Feedback in session is designed to encourage your client to discuss what was helpful about the session and what was not helpful. You also want to be able to give selective praise and positive reinforcement for the client's compliance with the session's focus. Also, problems in the relationship can be discussed (e.g., "I don't think we are understanding each other as well as I'd like us to; let's talk about what seems to be the problem in communication between us"). It is very important to attend to any process issues that could interfere with the successful implementation of CBT, but we generally reserve discussion of this for the end of the session.

Setting the Schedule

It's good early on to set up the full 16–20 session schedule with the client if at all possible, so that times and days of the week become "regular" for you both. Laying out all the planned sessions can be also helpful in reassuring your client that therapy will continue, even if the client is not responding yet or doesn't know how helpful it will be, etc.

Repeat the time and date of the next appointment and be sure the client writes it down. *We strongly recommend doing this as a regular practice.*

Home Practice

Try to set the specific time that the client will do the home practice, since increased structure and collaboration will improve the probability of the client completing the task. Home practice is ideally related to a theme discussed during the session or to a client's target complaint. Be sure the client writes down the assignment. Encourage questions *now* if it's unclear what is to be done.

Possible at-home assignments include:

✎ Have client work on additional target complaints, using the example of Mabel in the workbook as a guide, if there was time to do only **one** in the session. Ask that the client work on the second target complaint (e.g., "Do you think that finishing a goal setting worksheet for the next problem would be a good home practice assignment for this week?").

✎ If there are at least 2 measureable goals for therapy at this point, then home practice could consist of getting the client to start reading more about what therapy will actually be like. If the client's reading level is adequate, then making an assignment from one of the CBT self-help books such as *Mind Over Mood* by Greenberger and Padesky (1995) or *The Feeling Good Handbook* by David Burns (1999) is a good way to get the client started.

✎ If the client is very anxious as well as depressed, you may elect to have her begin relaxation exercises. For home practice, you might tell the client to obtain (purchase or borrow) a relaxing tape or a music CD that soothes her and ask her to play it several times before the next session and come in ready to discuss the impact it had on her tension levels during the week. It would also be reasonable to introduce relaxation exercises and practice them in session to get the client started on a relaxation program, if anxiety appears to be a serious problem.

Middle Phase of Therapy

Introduction

At this point, the client should be acquainted with the general structure and procedures used in CBT. The therapist and the client, working together, should have converted several target complaints into initial treatment goals and prioritized them by their importance. In the middle phase of therapy, the clients will develop the cognitive and behavioral skills that will help them address their therapy goals. The middle phase of therapy is typically the longest, and usually ranges from 8 to 16 sessions, depending on the clients' cognitive capabilities, the severity of their physical and emotional conditions, the availability of resources, and the complexity of their current treatment goals.

The middle phase is comprised of four modules that present cognitive and behavioral tools for coping with psychological distress: "Doing Tools," "Thinking Tools," "Feeling Tools," and "Communication Tools." Before the conclusion of therapy, the client ideally should be familiar with at least some of the techniques from all four modules. The amount of time spent on each module and the order in which they are covered will vary depending on the nature of the clients' problems and their characteristic ways of dealing with internal and interpersonal stress in their lives. See the decision chart (Table II.1) and the discussion that follows for guidance on when to start with the Doing, Thinking, or Feeling Tools modules. The Communication Tools module is rarely the first module, because it relies heavily on many of the skills presented in the other modules.

Considerable research done over the past 30 years has shown that as the client becomes more active, the level of depressive symptoms tends to decrease and the client is able to view stressful events from a different perspective. Thought and mood monitoring skills are then more likely to have a positive impact.

Typically, most therapists working with older adults start with the Doing Tools module because they realize that older adults in general tend to be less active than they were 5 or 10 years ago—even if they are not depressed. But for the depressed older client, this may be a very real issue—particularly for those who are not employed and/or who have no close family or friends to relate to on a regular basis. In that case, an appropriate first step is to get them moving and doing something. Behavioral activation is usually a good place to begin this process: by first having the client record what he does on a typical day and then building in more rewarding activities into his daily schedule.

Older adults with mild cognitive impairment (MCI) are also very likely to benefit by starting with behavioral activation, followed by working systematically to increase engagement in everyday pleasant activities or events. The presence of mild (or greater) cognitive impairment (regardless of the cause) can be determined through use of measures such as the Mini-Mental State Exam (MMSE), described earlier in this book. If cognitive impairment is severe, it is prudent to question whether CBT is the best intervention. Possibly, referring the client to a day care program for cognitively impaired adults, which includes sensory stimulation, structured activities, and some interpersonal interaction, may be more helpful in the long run than a course of brief CBT. However, for those clients with less severe cognitive impairment, CBT can be effective in helping them learn about what they still enjoy in life and how to problem solve barriers to doing what they want.

A final instance when the therapist would start with the Doing Tools module is when the client has multiple comorbidities (e.g., severe osteoporosis, and therefore is afraid of falling; unable to walk unassisted; pessimism about the future, coupled with depression; no family nearby but care is provided by paid assistants who also provide companionship; and no religious faith or belief system). Such individuals may not be able to initially tolerate the "probing" of their thoughts associated with using the cognitive tools. To ease them into therapy, and to instill some hope that improved mood is possible, we recommend beginning with the Doing Tools.

When to Start With Thinking Tools

For clients in situations they cannot control, cognitive reframing is an important tool to learn, as well as understanding the distinction between "adaptation" and "giving-up"—the latter is not what CBT is about. Learning techniques such as "positive self-talk" to encourage oneself (e.g., when a painful medical test must be endured, to say to oneself: "I've been through worse and survived, I can survive this time too") can be a very helpful cognitive technique to promote development of self-appraisals such as "resilience" and "positive coping."

Clients with strong schemas, for example, those who believe they are "no good, through and through" and have really failed greatly in life, may not be able to respond to anything but a direct engagement in cognitive processing techniques. On the other hand, one may want to consider starting with a behavioral approach, so some small successes can be attained early on, which will hopefully motivate the client to continue in treatment.

When clients have obsessive qualities and tend to be chronic worriers, beginning with the usual cognitive techniques may just reinforce their preoccupation with negative thoughts, as initially they don't have the tools they need to challenge these thoughts and develop adaptive responses. With these clients, we recommend starting with the technique of "thought stopping" to learn how NOT to dwell on their thoughts, but instead, how to distract themselves. When they have mastered those kinds of techniques, and the ruminative nature of thinking can be controlled adequately, you may wish to work with a more traditional cognitive therapy approach.

The Feeling Tools module includes relaxation training skills, skills for managing frustration and anger, and skills for establishing more effective communication. Clients who have severe anxiety in addition to their depression would benefit quickly from the relaxation training. Those whose main negative emotions are frustration or anger, rather than depression, would benefit from the anger management tools, and those whose depression seems most related to interpersonal problems would benefit more rapidly by beginning therapy with tools for better communication. It is our experience that once these "unruly emotional states" are brought under some control, and the client feels a sense of self-efficacy about managing them, he will then be more able to focus on the underlying unhelpful thinking patterns and belief systems that have fueled the negative emotions. On the other hand, starting too soon to examine negative thinking without at the same time addressing the client's considerable affective distress tends to undermine the therapy and may lead to premature termination of treatment.

Table II.1 Decision Chart

Thinking Tools	Doing Tools	Feeling Tools
1. When the client is highly functional, has already established some routines in daily life that promote positive reinforcement and bring pleasure, and when negative thinking is clearly influencing the client's mood state.	1. When depression level is high (i.e., moderately severe to severe). These clients may need to have some sense of success at the outset so that they are able to engage in treatment.	1. When the client has severe anxiety in addition to their depression and would benefit quickly from the relaxation training.
2. When the client's primary complaints center on situations cannot control, such as poor health, financial reverses, or loss of a spouse or close friend or pet.	2. When the client is not as active as he used to be. This is especially relevant for the depressed older client, particularly if not employed and/or without close family or friends to relate to on a regular basis.	2. When the client's main negative emotions are frustration or anger, rather than depression, and would benefit from the anger management tools.

continued

3. When the case conceptualization suggests strong schemas/deeply held beliefs that are pervasive and are significantly under-cutting whatever good might result from behavioral activation.

3. When the client has mild cognitive impairment (MCI), it can be beneficial to start with Behavioral Activation, followed by working systematically to increase engagement in everyday pleasant activities or events.

3. When the client's depression seems most related to interpersonal problems, begin therapy with tools for better communication.

4. When clients have obsessive qualities and tend to be chronic worriers. (Start with Overthinking section.)

4. When the client has multiple comorbidities and may not be able to initially tolerate the "probing" of his thoughts associated with using the cognitive tools.

4. More generally, when the client exhibits considerable affective distress, which will need to be addressed before examining negative thoughts in order to avoid undermining the therapy.

Chapter 6 | *Module 3: Doing Tools*

(Corresponds to chapter 3 of the workbook)

(3–5 Sessions)

Overview

As noted in the introduction to the middle phase of therapy, you will frequently find it is helpful to start by engaging the client in pleasant and doable activities. This is particularly the case with older clients who are more seriously depressed. Depending on the status of the client, you may want to start with behavioral activation or you may be able to bypass this section and focus primarily on increasing pleasurable activity in the client's daily routine. In working through activity monitoring and activity scheduling, the client's capability and motivation levels will become clearer. The first section of this module will illustrate activity monitoring, activity scheduling, and behavioral activation. The second section will cover increasing pleasurable activities. The last section will introduce problem solving.

BEHAVIORAL ACTIVATION

Materials Needed

- Copy of client workbook

- Whiteboard or easel

- Activity Monitoring Form

- Activity Schedule

Outline

- Set the agenda

- Review home practice

- Introduce activity monitoring

- Introduce activity scheduling

- Employ behavioral activation

- Summarize session

- Give mutual feedback

- Assign home practice

Activity Monitoring

Depressed clients are usually engaging in very few activities. On the other hand, as negative filtering is a characteristic way for them to misperceive events, they also may underestimate the number of activities they are doing and how positive they might be. It is important to obtain an objective assessment of what the client is doing during the week.

In session, write down the client's activities for the past week on the Activity Monitoring Form (see Figure 3.1 in the workbook for an example). Include all activities even though small. Then evaluate the following:

- Pleasure (P): 1–10 scale

- Mastery/Accomplishment (M): 1–10 scale

- Overall mood rating for the day

Once the form has been filled out for the previous week, review with the client collaboratively. Use questions such as the following to guide the process:

- "Were there periods of time when you experienced pleasure?"

- "What *kinds of activities* gave you pleasure?"

- "When do you have higher pleasure? When lower?"

- "Do you see any connection between your mood and your activities?"

Review overall mood ratings in relation to activities (or lack thereof). This helps the client recognize the link between activities and mood. It should help the client begin to identify pleasant behaviors or thematic areas to expand upon in the activity scheduling process (next step). It may be useful to graph the relationship between activities and mood (see Figure 6.1 in Increasing Pleasant Activities section.)

Activity Scheduling: Scheduling Pleasant Activities

If the client's level of motivation and comprehension is adequate, then use the information obtained from monitoring the past week to do activity scheduling for the coming week. Help the client develop a structured Activity Schedule for engaging in pleasant activities over the next week (see Figure 3.2 in the workbook). Remember to keep activities simple and achievable. If the client has problems with anxiety, emphasize that completing pleasant and rewarding activities can be relaxing and can reduce the level of anxiety.

Determine whether the client is likely to do all or part of this. If the client appears hesitant, then explore what might get in the way and think of ways to offset the problem. If it doesn't appear that this is going to be accomplished, suggest doing a simpler behavioral activation plan (e.g., "You know, this looks like a lot to do for the way you're feeling right now. Why don't we start with less to do and look after this week, and see how it goes?"). Following are some questions to use in your assessment of the client's motivation to complete the tasks:

- "Do you think it will be a useful thing to do this next?"

- "How do you feel about your ability to do all (some) of these things?"

- "How likely do you think that you actually will do these activities?"

- "Can you think of things that might get in your way of following the schedule?"

- "How do you think you might prevent that from happening?"

Behavioral Activation

Use of this simple procedure is often one of the best ways to get a client with low energy and low motivation to become active and initiate a process of change. If handled properly, this can lead to positive actions and an expectation of hope about the possibility of constructive changes in the client's life. Essentially, the therapist problem solves with the client to find just one or two things that he might do that the client believes would make a difference in how he is feeling at the present time. Once a decision is made about what these might be, the therapist helps the client work out the specific details of what he must do that will lead to a successful completion of an action plan. The inactivity of a depressed person often is due to a tendency to escape or avoid potentially stressful situations. This then prevents the client from engaging in meaningful positive activities that may resolve or minimize negative life situations. If you have chosen to start with this intervention, it's likely because the client is seriously depressed with low energy, little motivation, and few expectations of any positive change. In this case, it is necessary to start with one or two actions that the client can work on with high probability of success in completing them. The sequence of tasks is as follows:

1) Assess what kinds of activities the client is doing, how often he is doing them, whether he perceives himself as competent in doing them, and whether pleasure is obtained as a result.

2) Explain the rationale for engaging in meaningful activities.

3) Collaboratively work with the client to identify activities to work on.

4) Break any given task or activity down into manageable components.

5) Practice the strategies needed to complete the components.

6) Formulate a plan for implementing the actions to be taken.

Key Points for Utilizing Behavioral Activation

- A collaborative relationship is essential.

- The client makes final choices of activities (with the help of the therapist).

  - "We support that which we help create!"

- Complexity of activities must match client's level of energy, capability, and motivation.

- Explore client's readiness for change if this is not apparent.

- To engage client, it may be necessary to:

  - Review rationale
  - Explain power of rewards in contingency models

- Start with easy doable tasks. Early successes increase energy and motivation.

- Encourage the client with examples showing that completing small tasks leads to big accomplishment.

- Socratic questioning is helpful in eliciting feelings about the activities and the anticipated barriers.

- Often, however, it is necessary to suggest several strategies that will work and then let the client select from the group (i.e., use recognition memory rather than free recall).

- Finally, be creative in your questioning so that it is possible for the client to make the *attribution* that they are the responsible instrumental agent in completing the activity.

Breaking Tasks Into Manageable Pieces

At times, it is necessary to break tasks into small or manageable pieces in order to complete them successfully. Depressed individuals tend to think globally and often lose sight of this valuable lesson. Modeling this skill can be extremely helpful to them in learning how to resolve seemingly unmanageable tasks. With older individuals, using metaphors can often help energize them to engage in appropriate problem-solving activities. Statements like, "You can eat an elephant if you chop it up into enough little pieces!" can be energizing.

Exploring Thoughts and Expectations

At times, it is also necessary to explore the client's thoughts and expectations about completing some activity. If the client is having difficulty following through on an activity, ask him to describe or record thoughts about engaging in the activity. More than likely there will be distortions in the client's thoughts. You may need to help the client challenge these thoughts before you can proceed. Cognitive restructuring may be necessary (see Chapter 7 on Thinking Tools), but detailed work with automatic thoughts at this point potentially could be counterproductive. We recommend suggesting more helpful thoughts to replace them, and possibly doing some quick challenges like examining the evidence to determine if their thoughts are accurate, and then attempt to proceed with the assignment again.

Therapist Note

■ *Another important point here is to be certain that all the operations required to complete the activity have been described. As outlined in the section on home practice in Chapter 3, implementing the "four Ds"— Describe, Demonstrate, Do, and Discuss—is often very helpful when setting up a behavioral activation plan.* ■

If you started with behavioral activation after the activity monitoring, this is a reasonable point for the session to end and develop a home practice assignment. Following are some suggestions, but the specifics will depend on the client's functioning.

Home Practice

Assignments in this section might include one or more of the following:

✎ Have the client review the Behavioral Activation section of Chapter 3 of the workbook.

✎ Have the client monitor activities using the Activity Monitoring Form.

✎ Have the client follow through with activities on the Activity Schedule.

✎ Have the client choose a couple of key activities and implement an action plan.

INCREASING PLEASANT ACTIVITIES

Materials Needed

- Copy of client workbook

- Whiteboard or easel

- California Older Person's Pleasant Events Schedule (COPPES)

- Daily Mood Rating Form

- End-of-Day Mood Rating Form

- Pleasant Events Tracking Form

- Graphing sheet

Outline

- Set the agenda

- Review home practice

- Discuss the importance of engaging in pleasant events

- Introduce mood monitoring

- Identify new pleasant activities and have client complete the COPPES

- Have the client begin listing activities of interest

- Instruct the client on keeping track of personal pleasant events

- Introduce end-of-day rating for monitoring mood

- Use a graph to illustrate the relationship between the pleasant activities and mood

- Problem solve obstacles to increasing specific pleasant activities

- Summarize session

- Give mutual feedback

- Assign home practice

Therapist Note

■ *Depending on the client's progress, it may be necessary to extend activity scheduling and behavioral activation. If it's appropriate, then introduce strategies to help identify pleasant activities, in which the client can readily engage. This section is designed so that the client can get a meaningful experience of the power of pleasant activities.* ■

Importance of Engaging in Pleasant Events

One popular theory about the causes of depression emphasizes the functional relationship between depression and everyday life events. The theory reasons that when one encounters an event or maybe a series of life events that reduces the level of pleasure one experiences in daily life, one's mood is lowered. Remind clients of the downward spiral presented in Session 1. When mood is lowered, then level of activity also decreases. When level of activity is reduced, then there is even less likelihood to engage in activities that would be pleasurable. This tends to lower mood even further, which in turn continues to reduce our activity level, and so on, until the person is in a vicious tailspin that leads to a prolonged mood disturbance and the development of numerous other symptoms of depression.

In our work with depressed older clients over the years, we have observed this circular relationship over and over again. And just as often, we have found that if we can convince depressed clients to increase their level of pleasant activities on a daily basis, then their mood is improved and their symptoms of depression are reduced. If this problem is approached systematically, depressed individuals frequently can and do develop the skill of increasing their level of pleasant activities in order to offset negative life events and the resulting lowering of mood. Remind clients of the upward spiral presented in Session 1. Emphasize that building more pleasant activities into their schedules can help alleviate their depression.

Monitoring Mood

The first step to increasing pleasant activities is to learn to monitor mood more carefully, in order to notice subtle mood changes. Many clients will report that their mood is "just so-so," without noticing the gradations in between. The case example of Susan appears in the client workbook. Use this example (or a similar one of your preference) to demonstrate the relationship between different events during the day and the changes in one's mood. Often, when clients become overwhelmed by their mood, and they are unaware that they may be experiencing several different moods during the day, it is helpful to ask them to rate their mood at several key points during the day (e.g., upon awakening, at lunch time, at dinner time, and then at bedtime). Refer to Figure 3.3 in the workbook and point out the relationship between Susan's mood and the events that she experienced during different points during the day. In order to expand the client's knowledge of the relationship between mood and behaviors, have him complete the blank Daily Mood Rating Form in the workbook. Encourage your clients to pay attention to the events that surround their moods and record those events that they believe contributed to their mood scores.

Identifying Pleasant Activities

The initial focus of the behavioral activation section was on activities that the client has already been engaging in or has the immediate opportunity to do so. As the client understands more at the experiential level about the contingency of activities and mood, it is helpful to identify other pleasant activities that he might plan to try in the future. Employ the following strategies:

- Brainstorm with the client to learn of other meaningful activities.

- Use results from the Activity Monitoring Form.

- Focus on simple and doable activities; for example, courtesy gestures or contacts with vendors at a favorite coffee shop.

- Inquire what used to be pleasurable in the past.

- Use questions to determine what stopped pleasurable activities.

- If barriers are real and can't be modified (e.g., chronic illness), explore what might be good substitutes.

Helpful Hints

Older clients often have difficulty in coming up with ideas, because of the changes in their free recall memory, particularly if depressed. Structuring interactions with them so they can use cued recall or recognition memory is more productive and decreases tension and anxiety in the client. They also may have fairly fixed beliefs about their capabilities and interests that are counterproductive.

Testing Beliefs

A common problem is the belief that "I don't enjoy anything anymore." Your question might be, "Is that really true? You don't enjoy anything anymore?" A litany of possibilities can then follow from the concrete to abstract till you find something that counteracts this belief, as demonstrated in the following therapist–client dialogue:

T: How about ice cream? What is your favorite flavor?

P: Chocolate.

T: Oh chocolate! Do you not enjoy chocolate ice cream anymore? Not even a little bit?

C: Well, I don't enjoy it like I used to. I can't taste it like I used to.

T: But you actually don't enjoy it at all now? No enjoyment at all?

C: Well, maybe a little, but not like I used to.

T: Then you do enjoy it some!

C: Well yes, I guess I do.

T: Well now, how does that fit with your belief that "You don't enjoy anything anymore?" Does this mean that maybe your statement is exaggerating a bit?

A close second to this one is the belief that "I can't do anything anymore." A similar routine for questioning will usually show that this belief is not true as well. This helps to point out to clients their tendency to engage in all-or-none thinking, and it is helpful to give a little mini-lecture on how these false beliefs lead to self-fulfilling prophecies.

Rating on a Continuum

If clients have an all-or-nothing attitude, encourage to try rating things on a continuum. That is, an event doesn't have to be pleasant or not, it can be "somewhat pleasant." Or an activity can be shortened or simplified. The ice cream vignette is a good one to illustrate this concept. Most people like some flavors better than others. Setting up a scale ranging from very little to the best on a 1 to 5 scale will quickly get the point across. The difficulty comes in helping them generalize this experience to other stressful situations. The more you help them practice different examples, the easier it becomes.

Finding Meaning/Purpose

Exploring with the client his values, the rules he lives by, and what these mean to him often opens the door for finding important activities to include. Questions to ask include the following:

■ "When you think about your life, the past and the present, what stands out as being important to you? What are some of the reasons for this?"

- "Who are some people that you admire in your life? What did they do that made you feel this way?"

Adapting Pleasant Activities for Patients With Physical or Medical Disability

Older clients often have physical or medical disabilities that make it difficult to participate in some activities. These issues usually become apparent during the assessment. Determine what can be realistically expected on the part of the client and compare this with what physical resources will be needed to engage in preferred activities. If there is a discrepancy, then problem solve to find similar substitute activities that can be done by the client. Modify activities enjoyed previously so that the client can engage in them.

California Older Person's Pleasant Events Schedule (COPPES)

Some depressed individuals abandon pleasant activities due to feeling down or overwhelmed. On the other hand, some people may want to do more pleasant activities, but are unsure about how to start. In either case, it is important for clients to discuss the kinds of activities they like as well as those they would find quite pleasurable if they had the time. In order to obtain this information, ask clients to complete a questionnaire called the COPPES. (A copy of the questionnaire is provided as an appendix.) This questionnaire lists 66 events or activities that many older people find enjoyable. As the list is rather long, it is not important that clients find all of these activities enjoyable. For each item, it is important that they consider (a) how often they have engaged in this activity within the past month and (b) how much they enjoyed it. If they haven't done a particular activity, they should rate how much they would like it if they did get to do it.

There are several ways the information from this scale can be helpful to you and your client. First, as mentioned here, going over the list can help clients recall things that might be pleasant if they were engaged in doing them. Second, you can help them identify those activities that are maximally pleasurable (i.e., a score of 2 on how pleasurable the activities are or would be), but they are not doing them at all (i.e., a score of 0 on how often are you doing this). Conversely, you can help them identify activities that they don't particularly enjoy (i.e., a score of 0 on how pleasurable), but they are doing them often (i.e., a score of 2 on how often they are doing them). In completing this "eyeball" analysis of the scale with the client, together you may be able to identify several activities, which the client could start that would increase the level of pleasurable activities or decrease the level of those that are not so pleasurable. A third way the scale can be helpful is to identify general categories of activities that are enjoyable.

You can also formally score your client's scale (see appendix for scoring instructions). Computer scoring procedures are available along with a manual for use in interpreting the data (see appendix for more information). By using the formal scoring method, you can obtain a profile of the client's scores across the categories, and you can show your client how he compares with others his own age in terms of enjoyment and active participation in activities reflected in the various categories. Thus, for example, your client might see that compared to others, he may be doing lots of social activities that he doesn't enjoy as much as most, and he may be doing far fewer activities that reflect actual level of competence, which he truly does enjoy. Discrepancies such as these provide useful information for problem solving and planning changes in daily routines. However, as noted earlier, this scale can be helpful without the use of the formal computer scoring procedures.

Listing Activities of Interest

Encourage clients to use COPPES to inspire their own personal lists of activities to add to their lives. You will need to help them get started with the form in session and then ask them to complete the form after the session before leaving the office or as a take-home exercise. Completing the form immediately provides you more time to score it for the next session. You can suggest to clients that as they complete the questionnaire to start a list of pleasant events that caught their interest. The workbook includes a form for clients to begin their own list. Remind them not to be concerned about whether these activities are realistic or complicated. At this point, if it interested them, it belongs on the list. See Susan's sample list in the workbook for an example.

Keeping Track of Personal Pleasant Events

Completing the COPPES was an exercise to help clients become aware of the types of activities that they would like to build into their daily lives. They were asked to make a note of the activities that caught their interest and *not yet* consider whether these activities are realistic or complicated. However, it is important for clients to not only identify pleasant events that they would like to introduce into their lives, but they must make a commitment to actually fitting them into their schedules. For this purpose, clients can use the Pleasant Events Tracking Form in the workbook. Review the example form for Susan (see Figure 3.4 in the workbook).

Monitoring Mood: End-of-Day Rating

At the point when clients start increasing their pleasant events (usually after a few sessions), we have found that it is easier to ask them to do one rating of their mood at the end of the day instead of at different points throughout the day. However, devise a plan that is personalized to the client. See Susan's End-of-Day Mood Rating Form (Figure 3.5 in the workbook) that corresponds to the same days listed on her pleasant events chart. A blank copy of the End-of-Day Mood Rating Form is provided in the workbook for client use.

Graphing the Relationship Between Pleasant Events and Mood

Once the client has increased pleasant activities, graphing can be a good exercise to see the results on mood. It is often very effective to do this

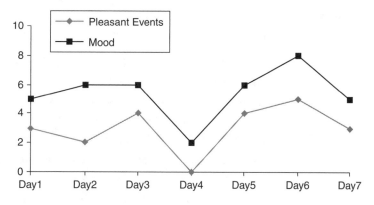

Figure 6.1

Graph of Relationship Between Susan's Pleasant Events and Mood Ratings.

with the client initially in the session. If the assignment is repeated, continuing this collaborative activity at the beginning of the next session usually increases client's therapeutic alliance.

Use a graph of Susan's pleasant events and mood rating to illustrate the relationship between pleasant activities and mood (see Figure 6.1).

Have the client look carefully at this graph. For the most part, as Susan's pleasant events increased, her mood increased. This suggests that in general, she could expect to feel better on days when she had more time for herself. Take a closer look at "day 2" on this graph. Notice that there were only 2 pleasant events performed, but the mood rating is a 6. Explain to the client that sometimes certain pleasant activities boost mood more than others. For Susan, visiting with her friends after being isolated for such a long time was so important that it was largely responsible for increasing her mood from the previous day.

The workbook includes a sheet to develop a personal graph for the client. The purpose of the graph is to help the client see the relationship between mood and daily activities. Once the client has data for daily mood ratings and number of pleasant events for each day during the week, we find that working with the client during session to complete the graph as a collaborative task greatly increases the client's involvement in therapy and usually facilitates compliance with future home practice assignments.

Problem solve obstacles to increase specific pleasant activities on a regular basis. (See next section of module.) For example, if there is a day of the week when the client does not have any pleasant activities, you should discuss the reasons for this. Work with the client to remove any barriers to regular inclusion of pleasant events in his life. It is *vital* for treatment success that mood monitoring and recording of daily pleasant events continues for a minimum of 2 consecutive weeks. Four weeks are preferred so that this type of behavioral activation becomes incorporated into daily life. Increased pleasant activities will assist the client greatly in maintaining a positive mood.

Our research has shown that four pleasant events a day keeps the blues away. These events or activities are consciously chosen and deliberately done; it is not enough for pleasant events to "happen" to the client. They must be planned into the client's day and implemented in order to be effective. Share the following motto with clients to help them remember this information.

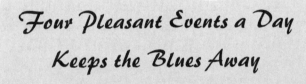

Four Pleasant Events a Day

Keeps the Blues Away

if they are Consciously Chosen and Deliberately Done

Home Practice

Assignments in this section may include one or more of the following:

✎ Have the client review Increasing Pleasant Activities section of Chapter 3 of the workbook.

✎ Have the client monitor mood on a daily basis using either the Daily Mood Rating Form or End-of-Day Mood Rating Form.

✎ Have the client complete the COPPES.

✎ Have the client list activities of interest.

✎ Have the client track pleasant events. If this is assigned, then also have client monitor mood.

PROBLEM SOLVING: BREAKING THE BARRIERS

Materials Needed

- Copy of client workbook

- Whiteboard or easel

- Problem Solving Worksheet

Outline

- Set agenda

- Review home practice. If client completed mood monitoring and tracking pleasant events, then collaboratively plot a graph at the beginning of the session to determine the relationship.

- Introduce problem-solving steps

- Have the client practice problem solving

- Summarize session

- Give mutual feedback

- Assign home practice

Introduction to Problem Solving

Problem solving is a skill that can be helpful in learning to use many of the different ideas and skills presented in this manual. We included it here, primarily because removing barriers to changing behaviors is most evident when dealing with concrete issues, such as how to increase certain specific activities or events in one's life that would lead to more pleasure or how to decrease other activities and events that increase stress.

Invariably, many events and factors occur that interfere with clients attempts to complete home practice assignments or otherwise decrease the likelihood of achieving planned therapy goals. Previous chapters discussed how unhelpful thought patterns lead to feelings of depression, anger, or being overwhelmed. Discuss with clients that when feeling this way, it is often hard to see potential solutions that will help change the situation into a more positive or a hopeful one. This section presents a five-step technique that will facilitate the development of more alternatives and options for managing a situation or solving a problem. It is referred to as DEEDS:

Define the problem

Explore possible solutions

Evaluate solutions

Decide on one alternative

Select another alternative

You may want to use the case example of Sally included in the workbook to illustrate the problem-solving steps.

Step 1: Define the Problem

The first task is to define the problem as specifically as possible. This step can often be the most challenging, as sometimes several different problems can be embedded into one. Clients need to sort out each problem and pick the one that appears to cause the greatest distress. If not immediately apparent, monitoring between sessions may be necessary to identify antecedents and consequences of the problem behavior or event.

Step 2: Explore Possible Solutions

This is a brainstorming step in which potential solutions to a problem are proposed. The key to brainstorming is NOT to evaluate each potential solution, but just allow suggestions to be presented.

Step 3: Evaluate Solutions

This step allows possible solutions to be evaluated based on any criteria desired. For example, clients may evaluate whether they have time to devote to one solution or another, or they may evaluate each solution based on money, energy, or how much help they would need from other people, and so on. As each item is examined, some of the alternatives proposed may seem unrealistic, and therefore will get a lower rating than others. In rating the options, the client may assign numbers to them or may choose to just use plus (+) or minus (−) signs.

Step 4: Decide on One Alternative

In this step, clients should select the first alternative solution and see what develops.

Step 5: Select Another Alternative

Step 5 instructs clients to go back to the list of options and select another alternative, or if necessary get more information about contingent events that precede or follow the problem.

Problem-Solving Exercise

Next have clients complete an example on their own. The workbook includes a step-by-step worksheet that instructs clients on how to problem solve. These steps include:

Step 1: Define the problem.

What was the problem? What did you need to solve?

Step 2: Explore solutions.

Remember, do not worry about the quality of each solution. Just write down whatever comes to mind.

Step 3: Evaluate and rank choices.

Start by picking out the most realistic, then the second, then the third, and so on.

What criteria are you going to use to rank your choices?

Step 4: Decide on an alternative.

What are you willing to try?

What happened?

What thoughts do you have about the way you solved your problem?

How are you feeling about your problem now?

Step 5: Select another alternative, if needed.

What alternative are you willing to try now?

What happened?

What thoughts do you have about the way you solved your problem?

How are you feeling about your problem now?

For Steps 4 and 5, you may want to have the client complete a 6-column Unhelpful Thought Diary (UTD) about how he solved the problem, if he is already familiar with this tool (see Chapter 7, Thinking Tools Module). If not, then you may want to refer back to this illustration when you are working with the Thinking Tools module.

Home Practice

Assignments in this section may include one or more of the following:

 Have the client review Problem Solving section of Chapter 3 of the workbook.

✎ Have the client complete the Problem Solving Worksheet.

Chapter 7 | *Module 4: Thinking Tools*

(Corresponds to chapter 4 of the workbook)

(2–5 Sessions)

Overview

This module usually takes between 2 and 5 sessions to complete, depending on the previous experience of the client in monitoring her overall cognitive capabilities. The first section focuses on teaching clients to identify unhelpful thoughts using a thought diary. Clients then practice challenging unhelpful thoughts and using an expanded 6-column Unhelpful Thought Diary (UTD). Some clients may need to address underlying core beliefs or "schemas" in order to effectively challenge negative thoughts. A section on overthinking is also included for clients who have problems with excessive worrying.

IDENTIFYING UNHELPFUL THOUGHTS

Materials Needed

- Copy of client workbook

- Whiteboard or easel

- 3-column UTD form

Outline

- Set the agenda

- Review home practice

- Introduce Unhelpful Thought Diary (UTD)

- Discuss rating the strength of unhelpful thoughts

- Discuss rating the strength of emotions

- Discuss identifying unhelpful thought patterns

- Review the list: Signals From Your Negative Headset

- Have the client practice completing a UTD

- Summarize session

- Give mutual feedback

- Assign home practice

Introduction of Unhelpful Thought Diary

An important part of CBT is knowing that our unhelpful thoughts create negative emotions. Yet, this process happens so quickly that clients are often unaware that thoughts occur between a stressful event and uncomfortable emotions. Thus, it becomes important to teach your clients to slow down thought processes in order to identify the thoughts associated with the stressful events that lead to intense negative feelings. Teach your clients to use an Unhelpful Thought Diary (UTD) to slow down their thoughts and to keep track of *what* they are thinking once they have noticed a strong emotional reaction.

Initially, older clients have difficulty in doing this kind of task as a home practice assignment. If you started with the module on behavioral activation, then your client will be familiar with the concept of monitoring mood and identifying possible contingencies of mood change. However, if this is their first introduction to monitoring, then it may take some time for them to master this skill. It is very useful to complete a few thought records in session to help them get started. You will find, for example, that many older clients initially have difficulty in distinguishing between a feeling and a thought. With practice, most are able to complete this task, and many can do UTDs effectively in their mind without using the form.

First introduce your clients to a simple UTD with 3 columns for:

1) a brief description of the stressful event

2) a list of the automatic thoughts connected with this event

3) a list of the emotions experienced as a result

Recording these three pieces of information on the UTD form will help clients practice noticing and monitoring the thoughts that immediately follow a stressful event. Emphasize to clients that they cannot make any changes in their thoughts unless they know *what* to change. With practice, they will be able to identify and change negative thoughts, which will improve their mood. Go over the case example of Jane and her UTD (see Figure 4.1) included in the workbook.

Rating the Strength of Unhelpful Thoughts

In order for clients to understand the impact that unhelpful thoughts have on their mood, it is helpful to assign some value or rating to these thoughts to indicate how strongly they believe in each one. The rating exercise can help them identify which thoughts are the hardest for them and which may need immediate attention. These ratings are also useful later in comparing how the strength of these thoughts has changed after beginning therapy.

Rating Scale

Encourage clients to use the scale 0% (not strong at all) to 100% (strongest possible).

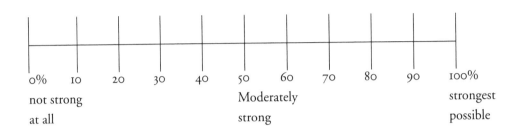

Go back to the case example of Jane and review the ratings for each of her automatic thoughts (see Figure 4.2 in the workbook). Explain that as Jane rates the strength of each of her thoughts, we learn which thoughts are more troublesome to her and may require immediate attention. For example, her belief that she will never get better is rated at a strength of 95%. This rating is an important one to remember because as Jane participates in therapy, since one way for her to measure improvement is by periodically re-rating the strength of this belief.

The Strength of Emotions

Likewise, it is important for clients to measure the strength of their emotional reactions as they record the situation. The range of the rating scale is the same, 0% means that the emotion is not at all present and 100% means that the emotion is completely present, or as strong as it could possibly be.

Explain that we can gain similar information regarding which emotions are the strongest, and we can also compare initial ratings to the later ratings of emotions as the client's thoughts change. Jane gives high ratings to her emotions of anxiety, depression, and hopelessness, with hopelessness and depression ranked as stronger than anxiety (see Figure 4.3 in the workbook).

As clients begin to identify and examine their unhelpful thoughts more regularly, they will begin to notice specific patterns in both the types of thoughts they have and the situations that are difficult for them. We may even go as far as to say that clients will recognize a particular manner or style to the way they interpret stressful situations. You may want to use the metaphor of a headset to explain this concept to the client.

> *Consider, for example, what happens when you are listening to a radio station with a headset. The station, or signal, will come in clearly if the headset is correctly connected to the radio receiver and positioned securely on your head. If the headset is not used properly, then you may mishear or misinterpret the signal or information from the radio. The same is true for the way we interpret situations around us and conversations that we have with others. Our interpretation of these events also happens through a kind of personal headset or a set of thoughts that we use to make sense of our world. When we are depressed, our headset is tuned in to a negative signal that interprets situations (whether stressful or not) in a negative way.*

A negative headset can be exhibited through different patterns, or styles of thinking, and a person can be employing several different styles at any one time. Following is a list of negative thought patterns that are common among depressed, older adults. The workbook also includes this list; suggest that clients mark these pages for easy reference as they begin to identify the kinds of thought patterns they use. People often find that some of these thought patterns fit them better than others. The identification of the more common thought patterns can be very helpful in later exercises of challenging and replacing unhelpful thoughts.

Signals From Your Negative Headset

Name Calling

When you attach a negative label to yourself or to others, you are engaging in a style of name calling. Often these statements have a blaming tone. For example, "I'm a loser," "I was a bad parent," or "My spouse is a real disappointment."

Obligations a.k.a. "Tyranny of the Shoulds"

This type of thinking refers to the rules you have about the way things *should* be. These rules are often unrealistic expectations that result in strong feelings of guilt or anxiety when not met. For example, "I have to have a clean house before I can do anything fun."

Tune in the Negative/Tune out the Positive

You recognize only the negative aspects of the situation and ignore or discount the positive accomplishments. Consider this example: If after making five pies for a party, one pie is a bit overdone and you think, "I can't make good pies at all."

This or That (No In-Betweens)

This signal refers to viewing a situation in terms of extreme outcomes. You see your choice of outcomes as "either-or" with no room for the options that fall in the middle. For example, "I'm a total failure," or "I never get things right, I am always messing up."

Overinterpreting

You have a tendency to blow events out of proportion or "make a mountain out of a molehill" when you don't have all the information. You also take the little information you have as "*truth*" without confirming its validity. This type of thinking occurs in three basic ways:

Generalization

You overinterpret situations, drawing conclusions with only a few facts. For example, you forget to write an important item on your grocery list and you begin to imagine that you are probably making mistakes in other things that you do, like you have forgotten to pay an important bill or you have no doubt messed up your checkbook balance and will be penalized for overdrawing on your account, and maybe you even have dementia!

Personalization

You assume that others have negative intentions toward or views of you. For example, if your TV repair man calls to say that he will be a little late, you immediately assume that he does not want to work for you and will probably just do a sloppy job.

Emotional Thinking

You use your feelings as the basis for the facts of the situations. For example, "I feel so bad, the situation must be hopeless."

What's the Use?

This pattern of thinking is common for people who believe that their thoughts or behaviors are not effective in changing their situation. The common consequences of this type of thinking are beliefs that your difficulties are hopeless. This pattern can also intensify depressed mood and inactivity. For example, "Whenever I plan an outing for myself it never goes as planned, so why try at all?"

Doomsday Thinking

You engage in doomsday thinking when you convince yourself that the future looks hopeless and bad outcomes are inevitable. People who use this way of thinking are often called "eternal pessimists."

If Only

The theme of this style of thinking is regret. Here, you spend time thinking of past events, wishing that you had acted or said something differently. People who engage in this style are often "stuck in the past" and find it difficult to shift to present issues or situations.

Continue with the example of Jane and illustrate the unhelpful thought patterns she is using by referring to the example UTD (see Figure 4.4 in the workbook). With this additional information, Jane is able to identify which signals from her negative headset she is using. It appears from this exercise that Jane is prone to doomsday thinking and name calling.

Practicing Completing a UTD

In the workbook, clients are asked to complete their own UTD using the following steps.

1. Identify the distressing event.

2. Identify the thoughts.

3. Rate (from 0% to 100%) how strongly you believe in these thoughts.

4. Identify emotions.

5. Rate (from 0% to 100%) how strongly you are experiencing these emotions.

6. Reread the list of Signals From Your Negative Headset and indicate which ones you experienced.

The workbook contains a blank 3-column UTD form for client use; this may be photocopied as needed. It is important to discuss with clients any difficulty they might have had in completing the UTD form. Remember that if you do not immediately address clients' facility with this exercise, you run the risk of them disregarding it and missing a very important step in alleviating their depression. Remind clients that the more they practice this exercise, the more automatic and easier it will become. Furthermore, it is important *not* to jump into challenging these negative thoughts after completing the first or second UTD. At this point, the focus is on recognizing that stressful events are fueled by negative thoughts and the skill to master is learning to identify such thoughts as soon as they occur, along with the patterns that they reflect.

Session Conclusion

This often is a good place to conclude a session, depending on the client's progress. More than likely, you will be doing a summary here anyway, and so it's easy to proceed into setting up a home practice assignment, doing a final summary, and getting feedback on the session.

If clients are having trouble with the UTD, they could identify one or more events during the week to which they had a strong emotional reaction and then make notes about what happened specifically. They could then bring the notes about the events to the sessions and together you and the client can complete the UTD form and identify the patterns of unhelpful thinking.

After home practice review in the next session, you could introduce the section on Challenging Unhelpful Thoughts. However, if the client's progress indicates that more work is needed in learning to identify patterns of thinking, you may have to delay this introduction. Nevertheless, it is useful to mention that the client soon will be learning ways to challenge and replace unhelpful thoughts to keep the client's expectation of improvement high.

Home Practice

Assignments in this section may include one or more of the following:

- Have the client review the Identifying Thoughts section of Chapter 4 of the workbook.

- Have the client record negative thoughts using the 3-column UTD.

- Have the client begin to identify negative thought patterns.

Materials Needed

- Copy of client workbook

- Whiteboard or easel

- 6-column UTD form

Outline

- Set the agenda

- Review home practice

- Present the steps to challenging unhelpful thoughts

- Review the list: Fine-Tune Your Signal: Changing Your Thoughts

- Introduce the 6-column UTD form

- Have the client practice completing a 6-column UTD

- Summarize session

- Give mutual feedback

- Assign home practice

Introduction to Challenging Unhelpful Thoughts

In our work with depressed older adults, we have noticed that as people practice identifying the signals from their negative headsets, the process of recognizing negative thoughts becomes easier. Once clients become familiar with the types of unhelpful thought patterns they use (this usually takes a couple of sessions), it is time to challenge the validity of these thoughts to determine if they can be replaced with more helpful thoughts. Next is a set of techniques to start the client off on the task of creating a clearer headset. Again, encourage clients to mark the corresponding page in the workbook for easy reference, as was done with the Signals From Your Negative Headset section.

Begin by presenting the two main steps to challenging unhelpful thoughts with the following dialogues:

Step 1: What is your headset? Identify your thoughts.

Write down your negative thoughts to see which patterns of your negative headset you are using to see the problem in a more realistic way.

Step 2: Challenge and fine-tune your headset.

There are several techniques you can use to challenge negative thought patterns and create a clearer headset. Some require you to perform actual behaviors in challenging your thoughts, and others ask you to analyze the thoughts from a different perspective.

Fine-Tune Your Signal: Changing Your Thoughts

Review the following techniques, and refer to the examples in the workbook of how Jane used them to help challenge and replace her unhelpful thoughts with more adaptive ones.

Action

Many people engage in specific behaviors to obtain additional information to challenge unhelpful assumptions about situations or people. Suggest to the client to try various actions such as asking friends for their thoughts about certain situations or practicing smaller behaviors before trying a larger task about which they may have high negative expectancies.

Language

As clients have probably noticed from recording their own negative thoughts, much of the negativity in our thoughts stems from the harsh language we use in talking to ourselves. Explain that we often create labels for ourselves or others without considering the true definitions of these words, or we believe that we must behave, think, or feel according to some "rules" of unknown origin. Changing the actual language from negative to positive or from harsh to compassionate will replace a negative headset with a clearer one.

As If

Recommend to clients that when they are talking to themselves in a harsh and negative way, to consider changing their tone and language similar to that of someone whose opinion they greatly respect.

Consider Alternatives, In-Betweens

When people think of only the extreme outcomes of situations, many in-between alternatives get ignored. Ask the client to think of a ruler that is marked 0 inches at one end and 12 inches at the other end—there are many inches in between as well as even smaller and smaller measurements.

Scale Technique

This technique is very helpful when we are "stuck" on a particular thought or feeling. Explain that the scale technique is designed to weigh the advantages and the disadvantages of maintaining the thought (or emotion, or behavior), to see which is stronger.

Examine the Evidence

Ask the client for information *both* that *supports* the negative thinking patterns and for evidence that argues against them. Most people can generate data "for and *against*" their specific thinking patterns. Over time, clients generally see that the evidence supporting their negative thoughts is less than the evidence against their negative thoughts. This process of gathering and examining the evidence "for and against" is one of the most effective techniques to counteract negative thoughts in older adults.

Evaluate Consequences

By now, clients already know that an overall consequence of maintaining a negative headset is depression. Emphasize that specific thoughts also have specific consequences. By examining the specific consequences for a belief, clients may find that they have less interest in maintaining it.

Credit Positive

Focusing on depression is a constant pull for negative interpretations; however, positive events, thoughts, or feelings do still occur. Ask the client to spend a few moments thinking of the more pleasant outcomes of events, positive thoughts she has had, and the positive emotional consequences that resulted.

Thought Stopping/Substitution

This technique is helpful for people who find it hard to extinguish a particular negative thought. When the client finds herself repeating a thought over and over, instruct her to try shouting "STOP" to herself out loud and then use distraction of some kind until she can replace it with a more helpful thought.

The 6-Column UTD

The UTD that clients have been using up to this point has had 3 columns to catalog the stressful event, the automatic, unhelpful thoughts, and the emotional consequences. As you and your client begin to challenge the unhelpful thoughts, the expanded version of the UTD is needed. This form contains 6 columns for the following information:

1. a brief description of the stressful event or situation

2. a list and rating of the negative thoughts that occurred in conjunction with this event and discussion of patterns that are present.

3. a list and rating of the emotions that were experienced as a result

4. a list and rating of the more realistic adaptive thoughts to replace the unhelpful thoughts

5. a list and rating of the former emotions (or new emotions that result)

6. A brief description of behavior that will follow. How will the client function differently now that there has been a change in her unhelpful thinking patterns?

Use the case example of Jane in the workbook to illustrate.

Practicing Completing a 6-Column UTD

In the workbook, clients are asked to complete a 6-column UTD using the following steps. For many older clients, this process is very slow-going. It's a new way of thinking for many of them. However, with time most begin to understand how to use the form. It's a good idea to help them with this in sessions, until they really get the concept.

1. Identify the distressing event.

2. Identify the automatic thoughts.

3. Rate (from 0% to 100%) the strength of each belief.

4. Identify the emotions.

5. Rate (from 0% to 100%) the strength of each emotion.

6. Reread the list of Signals From Your Negative Headset and indicate which ones were used.

7. Review the section" Fine-Tuning Your Signal: Changing the Way You Think" and begin to ask if your thoughts are realistic.

8. Replace the negative thoughts with more adaptive ways of thinking and rate the strength (from 0% to 100%) of each of these new thoughts.

9. Re-rate the emotions experienced earlier and/or list new emotions.

10. Describe how changing thoughts will result in new behaviors. What will the client be able to do differently now?

It is quite common for people to have difficulty with the first 6-column UTD they complete. It is also true that even if clients were able to come up with helpful responses to their negative thoughts, they may not have a great deal of confidence in these new thoughts. It takes time for the newer, more helpful thoughts to "sink in." Also, it is helpful to remind clients that they are challenging thoughts that they have had for a very long time. At this point, it is more important that clients become aware that beliefs they thought would stay with them forever can be changed. Emphasize that the way that changes can be made is through practice, practice, practice! Encourage clients to get into the habit of completing a UTD each time they experience something that adds to their depression.

Therapist Note

■ *Throughout the remainder of the therapy, you should continue to use the UTD form to help the client identify and challenge unhelpful thoughts when they occur in response to other stressful events. The more the client practices with this tool, the more likely the application of this tool will occur, nearly as automatically as the occurrence of unhelpful negative thoughts, per se.* ■

Home Practice

Assignments in this section may include one or more of the following:

✎ Have the client review the "Challenging Unhelpful Thoughts" section of Chapter 4 of the workbook and answer the summary questions.

✎ Have the client continue to identify negative thought patterns.

✎ Have the client begin to challenge negative thoughts using the 6-column UTD form.

OVERTHINKING

Therapist Note

■ *This section overlaps with topics covered in the "Feeling Tools" module in the next chapter. If obsessive rumination is an issue for your client, you may want to assign portions of that module, such as thought stopping, to the client at the same time she is working on materials in this section.* ■

Materials Needed

- Copy of client workbook
- Whiteboard or easel

Outline

- Set the agenda
- Review home practice
- Introduce overthinking
- Teach thought stopping
- Explain how to use "worry time"
- Summarize session
- Give mutual feedback
- Assign home practice

Introduction to Overthinking

Cognitive-behavioral therapy clearly emphasizes attending to how clients are thinking, but excessive thinking can lead to another problem. Sometimes, people can't put some thoughts, especially worries, out of their minds. You may find that some thoughts stay with some clients longer or will not respond to the kinds of skills that they have already mastered. Use the case example of Geri included in the workbook to demonstrate overthinking.

The Signs of Overthinking

Overthinking or "worrying" occurs when a thought or a set of thoughts stay around without any clear solution. Worrying involves "stuck" thoughts that may also cause increased anxiety or sadness instead of making one feel better. Sometimes, after worrying, a solution arises, but the time spent on this problem may keep clients from thinking about other important things. Discuss with the client what her signs are that she is overthinking. Also explore with the client whether she can identify antecedents to overthinking and what consequences occur after they have been stuck with the same negative thoughts for some time.

Advantages and Disadvantages

Often, this discussion will quite naturally lead to questions concerning what the client gains by overthinking and what disadvantages occur. Many older clients have had the experience at some point in their life that sustained preoccupation with problems seemed to facilitate problem solutions, which can lead to the expectation that if they keep mulling a particular concern over and over in their minds they will generate a solution. It sometimes can be helpful to explore the validity of that particular belief. For example, many exceptionally creative people, when questioned, will report that after they have reviewed all the pertinent available information pertaining to a problem very carefully, they then put it aside because the probability of a solution is higher when they are not continually mulling over the issues.

Many older clients may also have a superstitious belief that if they don't continue to worry about the occurrence of a particularly challenging event, then it is much more likely to happen. Thus, maintaining a continual flow of uncomfortable negative thoughts essentially thwarts more severe anxiety. Whatever the case may be, brief discussions about the disadvantages of overthinking may provide useful guides for selecting techniques to minimize its occurrence. Following are some techniques that have proven helpful with many older clients who are burdened with this problem. If these aren't effective, feedback from your client may help you introduce or even develop other strategies that can be helpful in reducing the frequency and intensity of overthinking.

Thought Stopping

This technique involves actively halting the worries and moving to thoughts about other things. One strategy to teach clients is that once they recognize that they are worrying, they should try to say "STOP!" out loud. This may feel very unusual at first but it can be very effective. You can suggest that clients practice saying (to themselves or out loud): "I am thinking about [the worry] right now, instead I want to think about [new thought]." This new thought should be repeated several times or worked out with a UTD. You may want to illustrate this strategy with the case example of Geri (see workbook).

Suggested Exercises

You may want to conduct either of the two following exercises with clients for practice.

1. Have clients pick one situation/topic and start to think about it and yell out "STOP!" after about 10 seconds. Clients often report feeling startled, yet this feeling can redirect their attention in order to either concentrate on this matter in a different way or think about something else entirely.

2. Have clients take that "worry" thought and try to write it out by attending to what they would rather be thinking about. For example, the client can write:

Stop! I am worrying about _____, but I'd rather be thinking about _____.

Encourage clients to repeat this statement several times to get a sense of what it feels like.

Worry Time

Sometimes, people feel better after they have worried about things a little. Worry time is a scheduled time during the day to focus on worrying. Instruct clients to make a worry list and avoid thinking about these worries for the moment. Then, they could schedule some time every day to look at the list and really think about these worries. It is important that clients *limit the time* to a specific amount, stick to this time limit, and plan something to do at the end of the worry time. You may want to give an example as follows:

For example, plan thirty minutes in the evening to worry right before a favorite television show. Look at the items on the list and think about each one, but stop as soon as your show starts. Many people find this technique helpful, although it may feel a little strange at first.

One useful suggestion is that clients set a kitchen timer; its sound will mark the end of worry time and remind clients to shift their attention. Initially, many older clients have trouble doing this. Many think it's silly, because they don't believe that something like this works. They may report that they tried it and it didn't help. It's important to get more details about what they actually did. Often, you will find that their attempts to use the strategy are done without commitment. You may have to do some within-session demonstrations, so that they actually experience what it feels like to control thoughts in this way. Some clients will admit that they don't see any real benefit from this. They might say, "What's the use of this? The thoughts don't really go away. They come right back again." In such situations, it is often helpful to explore whether setting up worry time has enabled them to get other things done more efficiently or more comfortably, which is often the case. Also, remind them that when they do this, they are actually controlling the occurrence of the thoughts, and as they have seen with other skills, practice will make them more effective in doing this with less effort.

Home Practice

Assignments in this section may include one or more of the following:

✎ Have the client generate situations that cause overthinking; these can be recorded in the space provided in the workbook.

✎ Have the client practice thought stopping.

✎ Have the client schedule "worry time."

MODIFYING UNHELPFUL CORE BELIEFS

Therapist Note

■ *This is an optional part of the therapy package. The decision whether or not to proceed with this section will depend on the severity of the client's problems, the client's progress in therapy, the therapist's decision as to whether this additional work would be helpful, and other logistical constraints, such as time availability for both the therapist and the client. Therapist and client should discuss relevant issues and collaboratively decide whether to add this additional section.* ■

Materials Needed

■ Copy of client workbook

■ Whiteboard or easel

■ Unhelpful Core Beliefs Identification Form

■ Core Belief Life Review Forms 1 and 2

Outline

- Set the agenda

- Review home practice

- Determine if client's core beliefs need to be explored

- Identify the client's core beliefs

- Teach the client specific techniques to challenge core beliefs

- Assist the client in replacing or modifying unhelpful core beliefs

- Summarize session

- Give mutual feedback

- Assign home practice

Therapist Note

- *This is an optional component of treatment that may or may not be used, depending on several factors:*

- *Client's response to therapy. Thus far in therapy the client's response may have been positive and additional work of this type may not be necessary.*

- *Client's willingness/ability to do more in-depth processing of their core beliefs. Some clients are not very sophisticated about therapy and may be unwilling or unable to engage in the more extended behavioral and cognitive processing required to change core beliefs. They may be satisfied with symptomatic gains and may see no need to go any deeper into therapy.*

- *Cost of extended therapy. Medicare or other insurance policies may discourage continued therapy of this type.*

- *Change in medical status or other daily life routines. Change in physical functioning due to medical issues, or change in residence (e.g., move to assisted living) may interfere with continuing for the number of sessions (typically about 8) required to do this work. If it's unlikely that the full complement of sessions required can be completed, starting work to modify or replace core beliefs may be counterproductive.* ■

Therapist Note

■ *In our experience, modifying or replacing deeply held core beliefs requires a commitment of 8 sessions or more. It will take at least that long to do the "life review" recommended here, to allow sufficient time to generate alternative adaptive beliefs, and to give the client the opportunity to try out these new beliefs in daily life and see how they work. However, it's important for maintenance of therapy gains to do this additional component of CBT in certain circumstances: first, if the person's depression is not responding well to the other techniques described in this manual (e.g., behavioral activation and thought records). Second, if there is some symptomatic improvement but there is a shared sense that the client could improve more with exploration of core beliefs, **and** the client expresses both interest and willingness to proceed. Third, if changing negative thoughts does not seem to be "translating" into much perceived improvement by the client after 10 or 12 sessions. He or she may be able to replace negative thoughts with more adaptive ones, but their sense of being depressed still remains. In these cases, use of this additional therapy component is warranted and in fact highly recommended so that more lasting improvement can occur.* ■

Getting to the Core

As you continue to monitor clients' automatic negative thoughts, whether it is through the use of UTDs or simply noting their occurrence in other contexts, you will begin to see recurrent themes that most likely reflect underlying core beliefs. Many clients can readily learn to identify negative automatic thoughts and develop rational reconstructions to counteract them. However, there are instances where the underlying processes are so strong and heavily ingrained that it is extremely difficult to help clients learn to challenge and change many of the unhelpful negative thoughts associated with these core beliefs. In such cases, little headway can be made until the client can identify and modify these core beliefs. This can be difficult to do, particularly in older individuals who have held onto their beliefs, unhelpful as they might be, for many years, and have developed habitual compensatory strategies to help them adapt and "survive" over time. For older adults, we recommend using a systematic and highly structured approach to facilitate the client's exploration of her core beliefs. The complete case example of Harold is included in the workbook to illustrate the procedural steps.

Steps in the Change Process

The following steps are needed to change negative core beliefs:

1. identify unhelpful core beliefs (UCBs)

2. conduct a core beliefs life review

3. explore other techniques for challenging and modifying UCBs

4. change or replace UCBs

5. use role play in session to try out new beliefs

6. assign appropriate home practice

Step 1: Identify Unhelpful Core Beliefs

As a first step, we introduce a series of questions for the client to respond to that (if affirmative) increase the likelihood that strong UCBs are present and are an issue for this individual. For example:

- Are there particular unhelpful or negative thoughts that continue to occur across a wide range of activating events or situations (e.g., at home, with others, often during the day, been present most of one's life)?

- Do many of these thoughts appear to have the same underlying **theme** (e.g., low self-worth, sense of inadequacy, belief that one has been a failure in life)? Typically, use of the "downward arrow" technique leads to such recurring themes.

- Have these unhelpful beliefs been occurring over many years? Generally this is the case.

- Finally, are these deeply believed thoughts perceived by the client as "facts" about them (rather than "points of view" that are negotiable)? This is usually the case with negative core beliefs.

Answers to these questions help determine whether continued exploration of underlying core beliefs is warranted. Assuming this is the case, you would proceed to help the client specify these basic core beliefs. The case example of Harold illustrates this process. See Figure 7.1 for Harold's completed Unhelpful Core Beliefs Identification Form. This completed form and a blank copy are included in the client workbook.

■ *Harold is a 77-year-old, divorced, retired man who came in for therapy due to feeling depressed. He is very articulate, but did not go to college. As he examined his unhelpful thoughts with his therapist, it became clear that he believed he was helpless to change anything in his life, including his feelings of depression. The issue came up several times in his thought records and in two "downward arrow" exercises. This thought also affected his therapy home practice. Harold very rarely completed or even started his therapy home practice, because he believed he could not do it right. Harold's therapist suggested that they examine his thoughts of helplessness as a core belief.* ■

In the process of discussing and completing this form, with the therapist's assistance in session and for home practice, Harold realized that he was raised as a "Watson baby"—meaning that his parents fed him, changed him, and put him to bed on a very strict, regular schedule. They stuck to the schedule no matter what and no matter how much he cried because he was hungry or tired at a different time. Harold thinks that being helpless to change anything at that time in his life (and up till about age 3 or 4, which was about the time he remembers having more contact with other children and his parents relaxing the rules, somewhat) may have been the beginning of his beliefs about being helpless, which continued into and throughout his life.

1. Which unhelpful thoughts do you have most often?
   I believe I am useless and helpless, I can't do anything.
2. Which unhelpful thoughts are the hardest for you to change?
   That I am incompetent.
3. Which unhelpful thoughts are the most emotionally difficult for you?
   I am a burden to others because I am useless.
4. Which unhelpful thoughts have you had the longest?
   Being helpless.
5. Which unhelpful thoughts seem the strongest?
   I'm no good because I can't do anything.
6. When you read your responses for the questions so far, do you see similar answers, or a theme?
   Yes, incompetence and uselessness.
7. If you had to state the theme you see in one sentence, or even one word, what would that be?
   I am powerless and useless.
8. When is the earliest you remember this theme in your life?
   Early childhood; I was a Watson baby.
9. How is that theme affecting your life now?
   I don't see any way out of my depression, but I hope the therapist can fix it. I don't believe I'm able to do much to help myself.

Figure 7.1

Harold's Completed Unhelpful Core Beliefs Identification Form.

Step 2: Core Beliefs Life Review

This step has two parts: (1) recognize salient life stages and (2) examine the evidence for and against the specific core beliefs at these various life stages. For better or worse, many older adults engage in reminiscence, which renders this a familiar technique to use to identify pivotal life stages and events that influenced the development of stable beliefs and value systems. It is important at this stage for you to assist your older clients to realize that often, life circumstances are responsible for the formation and maintenance of their UCBs. This insight seems to increase compliance with the many things they will be asked to do as they proceed in this phase of therapy.

To do a core beliefs life review effectively, you need to keep the process very structured. Older individuals are inclined to "ramble" when reviewing life events, and it can be difficult for them to stay on track. The forms we have developed and provided for you and the client's use should facilitate this process. We recommend their use, as opposed to simply discussing these issues (without any form of written recording).

Recognizing Life Stages

Once the client Harold (in this case example) was able to readily identify UCBs, he was guided to think about and discuss salient life stages (or "eras") in his life that marked turning points or included key life events that may have influenced or activated (or deactivated) the UCB. Important life stages vary greatly from client to client. For example, the case example of Louise (contrasted to Harold's) illustrates this point.

■ *Louise identified several important events between birth and 5 years that comprised one very significant stage in her life: mothers' death at age 2, father's remarriage at age 3, obvious conflicts with step-siblings and step-mother till entering preschool at age 5, when things began to improve. Louise began to be recognized as a bright and sociable child who was living in difficult circumstances at home. During her grade and high school years, she was an "over-achiever" despite ongoing family stress. This therefore was the second important stage that she identified in her life: school years, through high school graduation. Other important stages for her included: college and nursing school (where she felt very "challenged" and had difficulty completing the program); and her marriage from age 25 to 50, when she was happy, raised two daughters, and continued her nursing career on a part-time basis. Then her husband died suddenly when she was 52, and her subsequent years as a widow (her current status now at age 66) were very difficult and characterized by chronic depression. She thus identified a total of 5 stages in her life. In contrast, Harold had identified 7 stages in his life.* ■

Figure 7.2 is the completed Core Beliefs Life Review Form #1 for Harold. This example and a blank form are included in the client workbook.

Harold noted Seven life stages, which are shown here in some detail:

Life Stage 1

From: <u>Birth</u> to <u>seventh grade</u>

We moved houses—this was a tough period in my life. I told you I was raised very strictly so I never knew how to play and have a good time, it seems to me. I was always "on a schedule"—not like the other kids. We moved a couple of times. I think, so that was hard too.

Life Stage 2

From: <u>eighth grade</u> to <u>20</u>

Drafted for the Korean War. I did OK in school once we got settled and didn't move anymore. Actually, I did pretty well, since I'd been raised on such a strict discipline model. I studied hard and got pretty good grades. I didn't "rebel" and use drugs and that sort of thing. I'm sorry that I didn't complete college—I wanted to, but got drafted instead. I didn't know how to "beat the draft" like some rich kids did. I was always good with English and other languages in high school, so I was assigned to office jobs at first in the war. But then as things heated up, I was assigned to combat duty. I survived but the CO always kept saying that I was a "bad soldier" and didn't look out enough for the other guys in my unit. I hated the military and couldn't wait to get out.

Life Stage 3

From: <u>20</u> to <u>26</u>

Before I got married, it was really hard being in the Army. I was scared a lot and didn't feel I had many skills. I am lucky to have survived. Once I got married, it wasn't too bad. We made a pretty good adjustment I guess, but it was difficult initially since Kitty was pregnant when we got married. I wish we had gotten married sooner, when pregnancy wasn't an issue. In those days, if you were pregnant and not married, it was a scandal, so we got married.

Life Stage 4

From: <u>about 30</u> to <u>45</u>

Relatively happily married, but didn't do as well in my work as everyone seemed to expect. Lack of college degree hurt me as far as my work history goes. My wife complained a lot about money. We didn't have enough to send the kids to private school, which she wanted to do, and I often felt like a "loser".

Figure 7.2

Harold's Completed Core Beliefs Life Review Form #1.

Life Stage 5

From: about 45 to 60

Changed jobs, wanted to earn more money, wanted to be more of a success, not sure I was—tried a new field: computer science. Definitely not for me! I should have stayed in finance, where I was doing OK but Kitty wanted us to save more for retirement and an opportunity came up that looked good so I took it.

Life Stage 6

From: about 60 to 65

Felt myself going "downhill" at work and knew I had to retire. I wanted to wait as long as possible to do so, so my Social Security would be higher. I thought it would be a good thing and by this time, I really wanted to spend more time with my wife.

Life Stage 7

From: about 65 or so (when I retired) to now

I'm miserable and not adjusting well. Kitty divorced me at age 70. She wanted to do things: travel, etc. and we didn't have the money, plus I was too depressed. She decided she'd have a better life without me. That was the straw that broke the camel's back. I've been haunted by these thoughts and feelings from the past, since then. I look back and regret a lot of what I did and didn't do.

Figure 7.2 *continued.*

Examining the Evidence for and Against Core Beliefs

See Core Beliefs Life Review Form #2, which shows how Harold used this technique to help him get a perspective on his life history. In order to help the client systematically examine the evidence at each life stage, a series of questions are recommended, as follows:

1) What was this time of life like for you in general?

2) How strongly did you believe this core belief at the beginning and end of this stage?

The client is trying to uncover how much this period in life impacted the UCBs, so recommend that she start by thinking about how strong the core belief was at the beginning of this life stage and again at the end of this particular stage.

3) What happened during this stage that may have made the UCBs stronger?

Understanding the events of this time and the client's interpretation of these events is the primary focus of this exercise. Think about experiences that contributed to your belief system (examine the evidence "for" the UCB).

4) What happened during this stage that may have made the UCBs weaker?

Sometimes, our core beliefs are so strong that we minimize or completely forget things that challenge the UCBs. This can be one of the more difficult things to do in this process, but encourage the client to think carefully about whether there were any experiences during this time that were contrary to the core belief—examining the evidence "against."

5) What feelings and behaviors were associated with this belief back then?

Encourage the client to think about how her UCBs affected her life and behaviors during each of her life stages. For example: Were there things the client recognizes she did because of this belief? Where there things she didn't do, but wish she did, because of this belief? Were there any opportunities that were missed because of the strength of this belief, as it operated in her life at that time?

6) What would have been different if the client did not believe these UCBs?

This relates both to what the client perceives she would have done differently and to how others around her might have behaved differently.

7) Were there some reasons why it made sense to think this way back then?

It is important to recognize that sometimes we end up in situations where a belief that is "unhelpful" right now was actually **helpful** at certain times in our lives (certain stages). For example, a core belief that "the world is a very dangerous place" would be a very helpful belief for someone serving in the Army during the Vietnam War, even though that belief would interfere with their happiness if they held to it today.

8) **Encourage the client to talk to her "younger self." What would be said to challenge these UCBs? How would the younger self respond?**

Most clients can think of things they would want to say to their "younger self" that would help change their understanding for the better. Encourage the client to think about what would be said and even what advice would be given in the present (given the perspective now of many years having passed since these events/eras/experiences occurred).

9) **What would be thought or done differently if the client got to "do it over"?**

With the experiences and wisdom gained over the years, how could these stages of life be viewed differently now? If there was a chance to do things over, what would be done differently? The point of this is not to "cry over spilt milk," but rather to examine how to think differently about the past and to see if anything can be learned from these prior experiences that would be helpful in the present. Generally, there is much to be learned!

10) **How is the client being affected now by what happened then? That's a key question.**

Understanding the "carry over" of holding a UCB from the past is very helpful in challenging it in the present. Think about whether the conditions are the same as they were back then, and whether it helps to have this UCB even if they are. Mostly they are not, AND it's not helpful to keep thinking the same way about things. Examining the consequences of maintaining the UCBs in the present is the point here. The client needs to see that the "cost/benefit ratio" here is not in her favor if she continues to hold on to the UCBs. Now that she understands how these core beliefs have operated throughout life, she is in a position to modify them, so that more adaptive core beliefs will be present from this time forward. If the client has gotten this far in the treatment, she is generally very motivated to get to the next step.

Core Beliefs Life Review Form #2

It is recommended that you complete this form with the client for each of her important life stages or eras. This will most likely take several sessions. It can be helpful to select 1 or 2 stages that are "key" and focus on them, with less time spent on the others (if possible). In working on this process, and as this phase of treatment continues, it is also helpful to think about using other techniques in addition to examining the evidence.

Life Stage	Core Belief	Evidence For	Evidence Against

Step 3: Explore Other Techniques for Challenging and Modifying UCBs

Many of the other techniques used earlier in this manual, and "schema therapy" techniques presented by other cognitive-behavioral therapists, can be used to change the effect of the UCBs in the present. See for example, the work of Young and his colleagues (Young, Klosko, & Weishaar, 2003). Their book on working with schemas in clients with personality disorders presented a number of cognitive, behavioral, and experiential techniques that can facilitate the change process.

Step 4: Changing or Replacing UCBs

Now that the UCBs have been identified and challenged effectively, the next step is to develop alternative, more adaptive, core beliefs. Generally, this has been occurring (informally) throughout the process of completing the Core Beliefs Life Review Forms 1 and 2, and most likely, you as the therapist have been recording notes as to what the alternative schemas might be. For example, in the case of Harold, they might be "You are smarter and more capable than you think"; "You had a difficult upbringing, but overall, you did OK in life." or "You have some new challenges now, but if you have a different attitude, you can meet them effectively, just as you dealt with many challenges earlier in life." You might encourage Harold, and clients similar to him, to think along these lines: "I did the best I could, given my life circumstance. I didn't always make the right decisions, but overall I didn't do too badly." Or "I am over 70 years old now, clearly I'm not useless: look at all I've accomplished in my life." Or "I do some things very well: I keep the house in good repair, I pay my bills, I live within my means, and I have some money saved. I need to recognize my strengths and not keep focusing on my weaknesses. After all, I've got 10–15 years of life ahead of me, if I'm lucky, so maybe it's time to 'loosen up' and be kinder to myself." Developing alternative core beliefs that have credibility to the client is an essential aspect of treatment.

The case example of George, who believed that he was totally useless unless he was achieving success in his career, poses different issues. It is given in full detail in the client workbook; only key points are noted here.

■ *George is now in his 70s and long divorced, due to the grueling demands of his concert performance career—he never had time for his wife and had no children. He was a very successful concert violinist for many years. Now later in life, he realized that he believed he had value **only** when performing—but with advancing age, he was not able to do this anymore and had to retire from his profession. Then, this long-held belief (which was adaptive in some ways for him DURING his career, since it "drove" him to work hard enough to become as successful as he was) no longer "worked" for him. After completing the life review in detail, the therapist introduced two additional techniques that were very helpful for this client: (1) making predictions for how encounters with other people would turn out, which he then tested out in his everyday life and (2) using flash cards to remind him of the new adaptive beliefs that he had developed in the treatment. The flash cards included statements such as: "I have value as a person, above and beyond my technical skills"; and "It's taken me a long time and a lot of hard work and sacrifice to get where I am but I have to face facts: I can't do it anymore. Maybe—just maybe—there's more to life than being a concert violinist. I will have to find out in the months and years ahead. But at least now, I'm going to try." ■*

In general, flash cards (or other similar reminders such as Post-it® notes) can be used to help the client challenge the negative core beliefs in her everyday life. They should be placed where they can be easily accessed (on the refrigerator, in the car, etc.), and the client should be instructed to review them anytime unhelpful thoughts associated with the core beliefs occur. For many clients, this is an extremely helpful tool for promoting and maintaining change.

Step 5: In-Session Role Plays

These are useful to help prepare the client to "test out" new ideas about core beliefs in real life. In fact, we believe they are critical to success, since they give the client an opportunity to "test out" the new core beliefs in a safe environment. Clients also have the chance to see if they feel any differently now about themselves: Is their depression LESS when acting in ways consistent with the new core beliefs? Usually that is the case: Clients may be reluctant at first to engage in role playing, but once they do, they generally start to feel better about themselves and what they can do outside of the session to improve their quality of life. The example of George illustrates the effective use of role-playing to reinforce cognitive change:

■ *George had developed some new, more adaptive beliefs about himself and his self-worth but was not at all sure how other people would respond to him, now that he was no longer on the concert circuit. He expressed an interest in checking this out in real life but needed support and practice. An annual social event for musicians was coming up and he decided to attend and conduct an "experiment." He wanted to take some risks in his interactions with others and disclose more of his internal thoughts and feelings and see the results. The therapist agreed this would be a good opportunity to "collect data" to test his new idea (that he was a worthwhile human being whom people might want to spend time with). For a couple of sessions, George and the therapist constructed possible interpersonal situations and did extensive role plays, with both pleasant and unpleasant outcomes, while also noting what kind of negative thoughts George had and how he could counteract these. He planned to do some self-disclosure of inner strengths and limitations, but in the context of "being a scientist collecting data." George was able to distance himself from the interaction so that he could be objective in observing the outcomes. He did attend the event and was very surprised at the results. He singled out three people to apply his test. One person excused himself immediately and left the scene rather uncomfortably. George's immediate rational reconstruction to counteract the automatic thought that "This person sees the real me—nothing!" was, "Bob gets uncomfortable when people try to get too close. Maybe, he just avoids this like I do—I mean, did." The other two responded favorably, and both expressed an interest in getting together with George soon for another evening. George wrote down some of the comments and his reactions and reviewed these with the therapist to see how they supported his new belief about himself.* ■

This is an example of how role-playing in session can give the client confidence to test out new core beliefs in their everyday lives. Although it does not always go smoothly, no matter what actually transpires, the client can learn from it and with repeated practice, can "fine-tune" their belief systems to be more functional.

George's termination date was approaching, so the therapist spent the remaining sessions reviewing his progress and helping him to maintain the gains he made with a "survival guide."

More details about the "survival guide" appear later in this manual.

Step 6: Assigning Appropriate Home Practice

This is the last component of successful core belief (schema) modification. Clients need to work systematically through the process described here, with home practice assignments to match what is taking place in the sessions. By the end of this time, clients should experience that acting on these new beliefs improves their everyday quality of life. The more they experience this, the greater reinforcement occurs for the new beliefs, and the more likely they are to continue to be held.

Assignments in this section may include one or more of the following, spread out over a 6–8 week period of time:

- Have the client finish the Core Belief Identification Form.

- Have the client complete the Core Belief Life Review Form #1.

- Instruct the client to use selected techniques to challenge unhelpful core beliefs. The client can complete the Core Belief Life Review Form #2 to assist in this process.

- With your help, have the client develop new, more adaptive core beliefs to replace UCBs at this stage in her life.

- Encourage the client to try out the new beliefs in everyday life. Remind the client that she can modify the beliefs ("fine-tune" them) as needed.

Chapter 8 | *Module 5: Feeling Tools*

(Corresponds to chapter 5 of the workbook)

(3–6 Sessions)

Overview

This module will generally require 3–6 sessions to complete if done in its entirety; however, segments can be used as needed and can be interwoven into the other modules. For example, relaxation training exercises can become an integral part of teaching the client when and how to use cognitive or behavioral strategies. Particularly with highly anxious clients, including a relaxation exercise at the beginning or end of each session can help them focus better and including relaxation exercises for home practice can increase the rate of compliance with other, more technical home practice assignments.

RELAXATION TRAINING

Materials Needed

- Copy of client workbook
- Whiteboard or easel
- Tension Diary form
- Relaxation scripts
- Relaxation Practice Log

Outline

- Set the agenda

- Review home practice

- Introduce relaxation as an important tool

- Discuss awareness of anxiety

- Introduce the Tension Diary form

- Conduct relaxation exercise in session

- Incorporate visual imagery (optional)

- Explore other options for relaxation

- Help the client plan for home practice of relaxation

- Summarize session

- Give mutual feedback

- Assign home practice

Importance of Relaxation

Begin the session by discussing why relaxation is an important tool in treating depression. Strong feelings of anxiety often accompany depression. Many people report that increased anxiety worsens their negative thinking, creates significant physical tension, and intensifies any physical pain they are experiencing. Relaxation can be an effective tool to break this vicious cycle. We often hear people describe themselves as feeling "overwhelmed" by these emotions, unable to find a way to reduce their impact. It is also common for these feelings to be so intense that people find it hard to imagine a time when they were absent. Relaxation skills help clients gain at least some control over their anxiety.

Awareness of Anxiety

Ask clients about their awareness level. How do they know that they are anxious? Explore the following dimensions: specific situations, physical symptoms, and stop signs.

Specific Situations

Many people report certain emotional reactions to specific situations. Becoming aware of when these emotions are experienced will help prepare clients to take control of them. Ask if they are aware of certain types of situations that bring on intense feelings of anxiety, such as having to go for medical tests, waiting for the results of the medical tests, or anticipating that a particular family gathering or event will be difficult and stressful. Anxieties may also include fears, such as fear of enclosed places or travel (e.g., air, car, or plane), or fear that they will be taken advantage of (by family, unscrupulous sales people, strangers, etc.). The list can be quite lengthy for some individuals. Clearly, the more situations that the person is anxious about, the more important it is to address the anxiety as a problem in its own right. Focusing exclusively on depression symptoms in such cases would be doing the client a disservice.

Physical Symptoms

Physical symptoms—bodily tension, headaches, rapid breathing, and so on—also let us know that we are tense. Explain that these physical symptoms are typical signs of anxiety that we refer to as "danger signals." Spend a few moments talking with the client about his physical symptoms that are signals of anxiety and tension and note them for further discussion. Most clients judge their level of anxiety according to the severity of these symptoms so it is important to know the full range of symptoms involved.

Stop Signs

Explain that danger signals are the body's way of announcing that we must stop what we are doing to calm down and refocus our thoughts. When a danger signal arises, it is time to introduce a "stop sign," which is a behavior or a thought that will put the breaks on the negative feelings. Some examples of "stop signs" are taking a deep breath, leaving the room, turning the lights off for a moment, or a combination of all of these things. Discuss with the client what might work for him as a "stop sign." This should be something that will be easy for the client to remember and to do, while also being effective.

Therapist Note

■ *Remember stop signs have to be personalized: What works for one individual may not work for another. But the point is this: Anxiety will continue unchecked until it is interrupted, and using a personalized stop sign helps to do that.* ■

After the stop sign is introduced, the client should assess his tension level and do an appropriate relaxation exercise to reduce the anxiety/tension. Relaxation will help the client think more clearly (without the interference of the anxiety) and get "back on target."

Tension Diary

Using a Tension Diary is often very helpful to understand the sources of anxiety and types of danger signals experienced. The Tension Diary allows clients to record their most stressful times, least stressful times, and physical symptoms of tension. The workbook includes the case example of Mark to demonstrate the use of relaxation training. See Figure 5.1 in the workbook for Mark's completed Tension Diary.

Relaxation Training

There are many effective methods of relaxation, but you should be somewhat cautious in selecting exercises for older adults. This section reviews several relaxation techniques that we have found helpful and that seem to be acceptable to most older adults. We suggest a trial and error method of selecting exercises for clients. Remember that some methods are more appropriate for some situations than others—for example, a simple deep-breathing exercise can be done virtually anywhere, whereas listening to music or going for a walk can be very relaxing but requires more time and equipment (CD player, walking shoes, etc.). Most older adults welcome the opportunity to learn about a variety of relaxation methods. Many are already practicing some form of relaxation that may not work so well anymore or that may be too time or energy consuming to be effective at this point in their lives. It is good to review with clients what they are already doing and whether or not it's working for them.

Therapist Note

■ *It can be quite difficult for older adults with joint or muscular difficulties to engage in exercises requiring the physical tensing and releasing of their muscles, as is commonly found in the technique called progressive muscle relaxation. Therefore, that particular method, although very effective, is not generally recommended for use with older adults. (See an excellent chapter by Bernstein et al., 2007, for thorough discussion of issues to consider when conducting progressive relaxation, including when it might be contraindicated, and shortened methods to use that do not involve the entire body.)* ■

Tension Rating

In order for clients to gauge whether relaxation is helpful, we suggest getting them in the habit of doing a pre- and post-tension rating using the scale below (also found in the workbook).

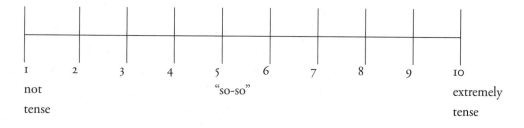

1	2	3	4	5	6	7	8	9	10
not tense				"so-so"					extremely tense

Talk with the client about what has contributed to the rating. Ask the following questions:

- "Why do you feel this way?"

- "What danger signals are you experiencing now?"

- "How do you know you are anxious?"

- "What kind of stop signs can you use?"

Guided Relaxation

We recommend starting with a brief, guided relaxation exercise that is quite effective with older people who are experiencing significant anxiety along with depression. Use the following instructions to conduct the exercise in session. Ask clients to first rate their tension *before* you start the exercise and then have them rate it again *after* the exercise is completed. At that time, if the tension level has not dropped, ask for feedback (What interfered? Were there intrusive thoughts? Did the person have difficulty focusing attention on the breath?). Try to find out what the problem is, then problem solve for a remedy. If there is time, repeat the exercise in session so that the client has an opportunity to experience the value of this technique.

Instructions for In-Session Exercise

1. *Sit in a comfortable position, keeping arms and legs uncrossed.*

2. *Keep your eyes closed and try to block out all external sounds.*

3. *This deep-breathing exercise is very simple: I will ask you to breathe very slowly, inhaling through the nose and exhaling through the mouth. Focus on your breathing, and breathe with a steady pace. To help you breathe in slowly, I will click my fingers five times—please inhale to that count, then exhale to the same count, if you can. If that bothers you in any way, let me know and we will shorten the intervals. If not, let's continue. (Therapist: Do*

this count for about 5 cycles. For most people that is enough to bring their tension level down to some extent, at least.)

Visual Imagery

Option #1

You can ask the client to use visual imagery as well and to incorporate that with the deep breathing. We suggest you do not do that until the client masters the slow, deep breathing. Once he is comfortable with the breathing, adding visual imagery tends to help the client relax more deeply. Before starting the exercise, ask the client to select a safe and relaxing place and to picture it in their "mind's eye." If clients have a problem coming up with something, suggest scenes, such as the beach, a lake, a location in the mountains, or in the warm desert sun. Once the client has decided on an image in mind, you can begin. The following are useful phrases for guiding the relaxation:

- *Imagine a (this) safe and relaxing place where there are no worries or cares or concerns.*

- *Now imagine yourself in that place.*

- *Gently keep that image in your mind's eye while breathing, all the while inhaling and exhaling slowly and deeply.*

- *Let all thoughts that float into awareness, float out again. This is not a time to think about things, but to just relax.*

For most people, this kind of visual imagery induces a state of noticeable relaxation.

Option #2

This second option is based on imagery and is effective with people who have a good imagination. A complete relaxation script is included here:

Make yourself as comfortable as possible. First I'd like you to remove any objects from your lap and to place your feet on the floor. Place your hands on your thighs. Don't cross your legs or your arms. Close your eyes, so you can't see the light and so you won't be distracted by what's going on around you.

Now breathe deeply, and imagine that your stomach is a balloon that you have to fill up with air. Inhale deeply again, and exhale . . . . While you're exhaling say the word "relax" (or any other word that signifies relaxation to you) silently to yourself . . . . Continue breathing as deeply as possible . . . always taking in enough air so you are filling up your stomach and then exhaling . . . .

Right now, notice where your body is most tense. Make yourself as comfortable as possible. Relax the tension in your neck, shoulders, arms, back, legs and feet . . . . Keep breathing deeply and exhale, saying to yourself the word that you've chosen.

Now imagine that you are some place that is peaceful and safe. Perhaps, you are on a beach or near a lake or in a meadow lying in the soft grass. It's a beautiful, warm day and you are alone. Look closely at your surroundings. What do you see? Miles of clean white sand? The cool, tranquil water of the lake? Soft, green grass and flowers for miles? Wherever you are, you are warm and comfortable and surrounded by beauty.

Imagine now that you are lying on the sand or in the grass with your feet stretched out and your arms comfortably beside you. Imagine you are closing your eyes, and pay close attention to the sounds around you. Listen to the sounds of nature. Do you hear waves or the wind passing through the leaves of the trees? Do you hear birds chirping? Listen to the sounds of your peaceful place. You feel warm and relaxed.

As you lay there, you feel your body becoming more and more relaxed. You feel at peace. All your bodily systems have reached a state of balance, of harmony. Pay attention to the feelings of relaxation in your body. Take a few moments to enjoy the sense of balance, peace, and calm.

Soon I am going to ask you to come back from your peaceful place, knowing that you can always go back to this place just by closing your eyes . . . and by breathing deeply three times Slowly leave your place and focus all of your attention on your breathing . . . Little by little you will leave your place, and tell yourself that you can always return to this place just by closing your eyes and breathing deeply three times.

Now I am going to count backwards from 5 to 1, and when I reach 1, I will ask you to bring your focus and attention back to this room. 5 . . . 4 . . . 3 . . . 2 . . . and 1. Open your eyes now and mentally come back to this room.

Additional Relaxation Options

Music

Most people agree that music affects their moods, although they may not have consciously chosen to use music to *improve* their mood, or to relax, specifically. Many older adults enjoy music and find it can be very relaxing, if carefully selected and if they know how to use the equipment needed to play whatever they have: audiotapes, CDs, music through a TV channel, or some other medium. Clients can even be encouraged to purchase a special CD or tape that was designed specifically for relaxation (or to borrow it from the local library). There are many commercial products available that work well for most people. However, this option is not appropriate for all older adults since not everyone likes music or has the equipment to play it, or knows what really will relax them. But it can be worthwhile to find out if they are motivated to give it a try.

Music can help greatly with certain tension-producing situations such as sleep problems. We have often recommended playing soothing music to help individuals fall asleep. (Also, when they awaken during the night, it can be helpful for falling back to sleep.) Music is also helpful to calm individuals with strong anticipatory anxiety, that is, who are fearful about things that are coming up in the future (e.g., dental visit for difficult procedures or having to take a trip alone). Music can be played with headphones, for example, in the dentist's office while the person is being worked on; it can be soothing "background" when traveling (again, if the person can use headphones correctly); or it can be played while someone is doing a difficult task (such as when a client finds that music takes his mind off of the pain of arthritis, at least temporarily, while gardening).

Walking or Mild Exercise

Walking (or any other mild exercise that the person enjoys) can also be a reliable form of relaxation. Again, it is not for everyone, since not all older adults can or want to walk. But for those who do, walking to relieve stress can also be a "pleasant activity" that might be greater utilized on a day-to-day basis. For those who do not care to walk, other forms of gentle exercise can be recommended for stress reduction, such as stretching exercises (often done to music), gentle yoga, Tai Chi, Qui Gong, or chair exercise programs. Classes can often be found in community settings such as a senior center (which would add a socialization component that can also be extremely important for the isolated and lonely older client). There are also many videos that can be played at home.

Religious/Spiritual Activity

For older adults who have a religious orientation or background, significant stress reduction can be found in prayer, listening to or singing along with church-affiliated music, reading religious or spiritual material, and/or attending a religious or spiritual gathering or church service. Again, this is not for everyone, but for those for whom it is part of their life experience, it is a form of potentially deep relaxation that should not be overlooked. For those not religiously inclined but for whom spirituality is a meaningful concept, learning to meditate can also be very effective for stress reduction. There are many varieties of meditation and many pathways for learning. In our experience, these methods can be quite powerful for inducing deep states of tranquility, and clients should be encouraged to explore them if interested.

General Tips for Relaxation Training

Many other techniques exist for stress reduction and relaxation training that are beyond the scope of this manual. Our advice is as follows:

- Learn what the client is doing now, if anything, and see if it can be fine-tuned.

- Teach simple deep breathing, since it is so "portable" and, for most people, very easy to learn.

- Work with the client's lifestyle to suggest other methods, so that by the conclusion of therapy, the client has a repertoire of several relaxation techniques that can be used as needed to reduce anxiety and improve quality of life.

Relaxation Practice

Ask clients to practice relaxation daily (at least once a day) to reduce their anxiety. Instruct clients to do the exercise *when they are tense* if at all possible, so that they feel some immediate benefit. The Relaxation Practice Log should be completed before and after doing each relaxation exercise. This is crucial so that even small decreases in perceived tension will be noted, and the client will be encouraged to continue to practice. For those clients who are not initially able to use a relaxation technique when they are actually tense, have them start out by setting aside *specific times of day* to practice, and frame it as "relaxation is a treat you can give yourself." Keep reminding the client that *practice* is needed to enhance the effects and that different methods will likely have different results at different times. Sometimes, the only effective remedy for anxiety/tension is to rest (to lie down or take a nap) or to distract oneself (escape into reading a book or watching TV). However, we want to reduce the number of times that clients use these "avoidant" coping strategies and instead encourage active coping by conscious use of a relaxation strategy that works for them.

Relaxation can also be used to prepare clients for an upcoming stressful event. For example, if visits to a particular family member are stressful, encourage the client to spend a few moments in his "relaxation spot" prior to the visit. In addition, clients may want to try relaxation exercises as a nice way to start the day, even if they are not in a high stress moment. Relaxation can also create a calm break to refocus throughout the day.

Often, clients expect their tension to decrease more than it does after their first few practices. Remind clients that the more relaxation is practiced, the more relaxed they will feel immediately following the exercise. Also, with increased practice, there will be a decrease in the time it takes to reach a relaxed state. Some people report that their bodies and minds become completely relaxed by the first deep breath! Encourage the use of the Relaxation Practice Log in the workbook to gauge progress.

Home Practice

Assignments in this section may include one or more of the following:

✎ Have the client complete the Tension Diary in the workbook *at least once* each day, preferably every time he experiences significant anxiety.

✎ Have the client practice the selected relaxation exercise on a daily basis and record his efforts on the Relaxation Practice Log in the workbook.

✎ Have the client bring to the next session problems he is having with relaxation. (Does relaxation "work" like it is supposed to? If not, you need to make time on the agenda to discuss this with the client and try to problem solve, so that the method is more effective in the future.)

✎ Caution the client that at first, change in perceived stress or tension may be *small*; this will improve over time as he masters the techniques and develops more of a variety of methods to use.

IMAGERY AS A TOOL FOR NEGATIVE THOUGHTS AND STRESS MANAGEMENT

Materials Needed

■ Copy of client workbook

■ Whiteboard or easel

■ 6-column UTD

Outline

- Set the agenda

- Review home practice

- Introduce imagery as a tool

- Have the client identify negative beliefs through imagery

- Have the client challenge negative beliefs through imagery

- Discuss imagery for stress management and effective communication

- Summarize session

- Give mutual feedback

- Assign home practice

Introduction to Imagery

Imagery is another tool to manage intense feelings: A "picture" of the stressful situation and its possible solutions are created in one's mind. The visual imagery exercise in the Relaxation Training section of this module demonstrated one type of imagery. Recall that this exercise asked clients to select a safe place they could visit for a short while in their imaginations. These same visualization skills can help challenge client's perceptions of the outcomes of stressful situations and manage intense emotions.

Identifying Negative Beliefs Through Imagery

Imagery can be used to identify negative beliefs. Guide the client through the following steps.

1. *Think about a particular situation that produces intense, negative emotions. Briefly describe that event.*

2. *What emotions are present?*

3. *Now sit back, placing arms and legs in a comfortable position, and imagine the situation. Try to capture all of the components of the situation: the people, the sights, the sounds, the colors, etc. Try to determine what is specifically problematic; isolate the thoughts that occur.*

Therapist Note

▪ *The intensity of the images can cause clients to "revisit" the upsetting situation. If so, encourage them to think of some calming images before continuing with the exercise.* ▪

Instruct clients to record the thoughts about the stressful situation recalled through the imagery exercise on a UTD. Review the negative thoughts, and examine the evidence for and against them. Then have clients rate how strongly they believe these outcomes will occur (from 0% to 100%).

Challenging Negative Beliefs Through Imagery

Next ask clients if they can replace the unhelpful beliefs in column 2 of the UTD with more helpful ones (column 4). Work with them until this is accomplished, and check their feelings at this point. Instruct clients to record any changes in their emotions considering their new perceptions (column 5). Then, ask clients to consider what they will do differently in similar situations (column 6).

Now instruct clients to return to imagining the situation, this time picturing the outcome differently as they now predict it will happen. Elicit a description of this outcome. Is the original negative outcome as likely as it was before challenging the negative thoughts? Have clients rate how strongly they believe in their original outcome at this moment (from 0% to 100%), and how strongly they believe in the new outcome. Ideally, the new outcome will be rated as more likely than the negative outcome believed previously. If not, return to the thoughts and images, and continue to gently challenge them and develop alternative responses and new possible outcomes, until the situation has become less "emotionally charged" and the client has more confidence in his ability to manage it effectively if or when it occurs again.

Imagery for Stress Management and Effective Communication

Imagery can also be useful in helping clients to prepare for a stressful event. For example, if a client becomes anxious about meeting with someone, encourage use of the imagery exercise to practice and to plan the kinds of things he would like to say. Imagery skills also come in handy when clients want to practice being assertive before they are placed in a "face-to-face" situation. See the next chapter on communication tools. Finally, imagery can be incorporated when teaching clients how to communicate more effectively with people with whom they have difficulty communicating.

Home Practice

 Assignments in this section may include one or more of the following:

 Have the client use imagery to identify and challenge negative beliefs.

Have the client practice imagery for stress management/effective communication.

MANAGEMENT OF FRUSTRATION AND ANGER

Materials Needed

- Copy of client workbook

- Whiteboard or easel

- ABC Form

- ABC (Stop) D Form

Outline

- Set the agenda

- Review home practice

- Help the client identify sources of frustration and anger

- Teach the client to defuse anger or frustration through relaxation training

- Introduce steps to coping with an unchangeable situation

- Assign home practice

- Summarize session

Sources of Frustration and Anger

Many older people experience feelings of frustration or anger associated with their depression. Some report going "back and forth" between feeling sad and feeling irritable or frustrated, while for others, frustration is *the* primary negative emotion of which they are aware. To frame interventions appropriately, it is helpful to understand the many potential sources of frustration and anger for older adults.

Lack of Knowledge

One source of frustration and anger is lack of knowledge about common negative emotions that people tend to experience more of as they age. Often, clients do not realize that a certain amount of depression, frustration, or anger may be very appropriate, given their circumstances. For example, it's reasonable to become frustrated when one's adult son or daughter always seems "too busy" to visit or call, or when one's phone calls to the doctor's office are not returned promptly and courteously. However, these kinds of feelings become "problems" when they are out of proportion to the situation or become chronic and intense. For example, it may become difficult to have a positive contact with an adult child because of so much built-up anger and frustration over time from past rejections, and this in turn may lead to further distancing between parent and adult child.

Negative Thoughts and Attitudes About Oneself and the World

Many older adults who have high levels of anger and frustration have strong negative views about themselves. Often, they see themselves as a failure for not living up to unrealistically high expectations formed earlier in life. For some individuals, this turns into anger rather than into classic depression. Similarly, the client can become angry at how the world "let me down"; clients with a sense of "entitlement" often express their disappointments with anger rather than depression.

Skill Deficits

Older adults who do not know how to manage their feelings of anger and/or frustration and disappointment effectively may find that these feelings increase over time and after awhile, may "take over" so that the person is chronically irritable. This generally has a negative impact on those around the client, who often withdraw—sometimes out of fear but more often because it's unpleasant to be around a person who is chronically angry. This in turn reinforces the client's feeling that no one cares, or the "world is out to get me," and that in turn tends to increase depressive feelings. When the client does not know how to communicate feelings effectively, he may passively suppress anger or may vent feelings in an aggressive manner, neither of which are particularly effective for problem solving. Thus, a "vicious cycle" is created where anger and depression feed into one another. See the next chapter on communication tools.

Lack of Control

Anger is also a common response to dealing with people or situations over which the client has no control, but believes he *should* have control.

For example, if the older adult is volunteering at a school to help children learn to read each week, but there's a new group of children every time, despite requesting a more stable group, the client may become upset that his expressed wishes are not being respected or listened to. But instead of trying to discuss this with the appropriate people in charge, the client may quit altogether and leave angry that he was not appreciated. This has many negative repercussions, not the least of which is that the client becomes *more* angry since he now perceives he has in fact been rejected by the very system with which he was trying to be involved. Frequently, this type of situation leads to increased depression. Again, we wish to emphasize the importance of working with the client to develop and practice and to use effective communication skills, as this is often a critical part of the overall skill training that is needed for learning to manage frustration and respond more effectively.

Of course there are many circumstances in life over which an individual has little or no control; most people adapt to those kinds of situations (e.g., chronic debilitating illness) but some do not and continue to insist that they should be "in charge" of the world and of what happens to them. This viewpoint will necessarily lead to increased feelings of anger and frustration that can become very entrenched over time.

Defusing Anger or Frustration Through Relaxation Training

What typically happens to the client who becomes angry or frustrated frequently? The body tenses up—for example, tension may be consciously experienced in the jaw, neck, and shoulder areas, which seem particularly vulnerable to this feeling state. Usually, certain movements characterize the person (such as walking quickly, counting aloud, clenching the fists, standing in a certain challenging or aggressive pose, etc.). In addition, the person often uses certain verbal expressions (e.g., curse or swear words, other forms of negative, critical language).

Taken together, it is usually apparent, from the words and actions of the client, that he is very angry at the moment. When this occurs in session, you are advised to return to the relaxation section of this module in order to be reminded of the various methods for *relaxation training* (e.g., deep breathing). It is recommended that a simple, brief relaxation exercise be done in session to help the client learn that negative feelings such as anger can be reduced with practice. The Tension Diary should be completed before and after the relaxation exercise also, to measure if it was effective.

Coping With an Unchangeable Situation

When "unchangeable" situations are the root cause of strong anger, which occurs often in the lives of older clients, it is helpful to point out to the client that there are three possible responses to a situation over which one has little or no control:

- Assertively try to change the situation

- Leave the situation if you can

- Adapt yourself so that you can live with it and feel less frustrated about it

While the first two solutions are possible in some instances, more often than not, the client must learn to adapt so that his level of anger is reduced, resulting in less psychological distress for the individual.

In order to help the client learn to manage strong feelings of anger and frustration, he must learn several steps:

1) Recognize that the anger is getting out of hand. This includes being aware of danger signals and which stop signs need to be employed in order to dampen the negative feelings.

2) Identify the thoughts that fuel the anger.

3) Evaluate these thoughts and attempt to see the event or situation from different angles.

4) Change the thinking, that is, develop more helpful or adaptive thoughts that promote positive coping.

5) Behave or do things *differently* in the situation that typically provokes the anger or frustration, thus leading to a different outcome.

Step 1: Recognize That the Anger Is Getting Out of Hand

To recognize that the anger is getting out of hand, clients need to learn about "danger signals" and "stop signs," similar to those used with anxiety discussed earlier.

Danger Signals

Danger signals are the particular changes in the body that occur when feelings of anger are rising, such as breathing heavily, heart feels like its racing, and sweating. Clients might make statements like "I feel a rush of blood to my head," or "My throat is tightening up." Everyone has their own unique danger signals, and clients readily understand what you are referring to when you ask them to identify theirs.

Stop Signs

Stop signs are strong visual images that interrupt the negative feelings and the "train of thoughts" long enough to enable the client to gain cognitive control. When used correctly, individualized stop signs enable the client to take a short breather when feeling overwhelmed by negative emotions or the physical sensations associated with them. Stop signs are mental images that make the client STOP & THINK. To be effective, they need to be powerful, meaningful to the individual, and shown to be effective in interrupting negative feelings. For example, many people think of the traditional red STOP sign they encounter many times each day while driving. If they are good drivers, they will always stop at that sign. But for some clients, this image is not strong enough: They might need to visualize a red hot fire and see themselves pulling back from it, or visualize themselves at the edge of a waterfall where their natural instinct is to stop and not go any further; or they might imagine a horse rearing up and find themselves getting out of the way and maybe shouting "whoa" to tame the horse; or they might envision a poison sign on a label or a KEEP OUT sign on property that has been boarded up. The point is that whatever is both dramatic and meaningful to the client is what he should be encouraged to use.

Relaxation Training

For most clients, in addition to developing and implementing the stop signs, it is a good idea to pair or introduce sequentially the use of relaxation techniques to help calm the body and the mind. For example, doing the simple deep-breathing relaxation exercise described earlier can be very helpful for some individuals, who need to learn how to calm down physically so that they can then examine their thoughts. For other clients, stop signs in themselves are enough. This has to be determined empirically with each individual.

To make sure the client understands these points, you want to work with him to write out the danger signals (reactions) and stop signs (visual images) that occur when he thinks back to an anger-provoking situation (possibly already recorded in the Unhelpful Thought Diary). Once the client sees how identifying danger signals and employing stop signs are effective in session, then they can be assigned for home practice.

Step 2: Identify the Thoughts That Fuel the Anger

To help the client recognize thoughts that fuel his anger refer to the A-B-C model:

Action: **a**ction or situation that is creating or fueling the frustration

Belief: **b**eliefs or thoughts about the situation that are making me upset

Consequences: **c**onsequences in terms of my feelings (rated for intensity) in reaction to this situation

In session and for home practice, the client should complete A-B-C Forms to help him "tune in" to what he is thinking.

Step 3: Evaluate Thoughts and Attempt to See the Situation From Different Angles

We want the client to evaluate the thoughts that fuel anger and to see the situation from a different perspective. In order to do this, the client must first learn to *stop* (interfere with) his negative emotional responses.

The client cannot think clearly until the strong negative emotions are in check, as discussed earlier. At this point, it is helpful to discuss with the client the fact that strong emotions can be like a steam locomotive: Once you begin to feel them, they slowly grow and gradually develop a lot of momentum. Generally, the thoughts associated with these feelings occur so "automatically" that they are difficult to identify or modify. Emphasize that like speeding trains, strong emotional responses are hard to stop. However, the client can learn to do so, and in fact must learn how to do this, or else he will not be able to develop alternative thoughts and/or more adaptive behaviors.

Clearly, it takes practice to develop these skills, but we do not recommend going on to the next step (changing negative thinking by developing more adaptive responses) until this step is mastered. By first learning some tools for gaining control of the negative emotions, clients will be in a much better position to challenge the negative thoughts since they will be operating from their minds (not their guts). See the example of Bob included in the workbook.

Step 4: Change the Thinking

This step involves developing more helpful or adaptive thoughts that promote positive coping. Present the following instructions to the client:

1. Ask yourself (out loud or in your mind): Is this *always* the right way to perceive or to respond to this situation? Or is there a time when it's not? Think back to prior experiences and compare.

2. Ask yourself: What is the *evidence* supporting my point of view? What is the evidence "for" and "against" my beliefs? *Listen* to the evidence you tell yourself so that you can come up with a more balanced view. Be honest with yourself.

3. Ask yourself: Are there alternative explanations or possibilities to consider?

Refer to the case example of Bob included in the workbook to demonstrate the above.

Once the client has asked and answered these kinds of questions in his mind or out loud in session, the final two parts of this process involve:

- learning to *replace* the negative thoughts with more adaptive ones, and

- thinking about a better course of *action* instead of continuing to do the more "automatic" response

Again, refer to the case example of Bob to illustrate this process. The fact that this new behavior of Bob's "works" (gets the desired result) is something important to note: This kind of reinforcement tends to strengthen the likelihood that this behavior will be repeated.

Step 5: Behave or Do Things Differently

In situations that typically provoke the client's anger/frustration, it is crucial that the coping approach leads to new behaviors and better outcomes. You may want to use the case example of Mary included in the workbook to illustrate this process.

A-B-C (Stop) D

The A-B-C (Stop) D model is as follows: A (Action) leads to B (Beliefs) leads to C (Consequences), add in the STOP SIGN, and then go to D (what are you going to do differently now, now that the emotions are under control?). We found that by linking this model to *action* at the end, we increase the likelihood that it will be used by the client. So "D" stands for taking time to stop and think. Share the following steps with the client:

1) DO consider other possibilities for what you are thinking.

2) DO come up with alternative ways to respond to the situation that is making you upset.

3)   DO take advantage of your ability to reason things out.

4)   THEN ACT.

Clients will find that these steps slow down the "automatic" processing enough so that they can regain control and stop themselves from behaving in ways that they will only regret.

Other Challenging Techniques

Helpful thought challenges for angry clients include the following two techniques.

Keeping Things in Perspective: Teach clients to try and "keep things in perspective"—nothing is all good or all bad. It is helpful to remind them that often when in a tough situation, we think that it won't improve but the fact is that things change. "What happens today will not happen forever. I can make it through today" can be a helpful reframe.

Positive Self-Statements: When "mental filtering" is going on, the client tunes out the positive (e.g., Bob did not appreciate that he had gotten past the hurdle of getting an appointment, the waiting room was not full, or that he was "in the queue" to be seen) and focuses on the negative: (e.g., "Why do I have to wait again, why can't they schedule things right so they see me on time? I try to be on time everywhere I go"), we recommend teaching the client to affirm the positive. This involves learning to come up, and use, *positive self-statements* (some call them "affirmations") that help the client to reframe. It can be very helpful for clients to write these statements down on Post-its® in session. For home practice, instruct clients to put the Post-its around the house or in car or in purse and review them regularly. With Bob, for example, he was taught to say to himself such statements as, "I have my flaws (flying off the handle too easily), but I also have my strengths. I'm not going to beat myself up over this. I can figure out what else to do so the situation cools down. I've got a good brain, and I'm going to use it."

Summary

To summarize the steps involved in anger management, we provide a consolidation of several different skills presented in this program, as well as some of the unique content presented in this section of the manual. These steps include the following:

1. Recognize the situations that result in an emotional reaction of anger.

2. Recognize the danger signals (i.e., How does the body feel?).

3. Engage in an activity to physically calm down, such as relaxation, breathing slowly, or even exercise.

4. Use thinking tools to identify and modify the automatic thoughts that lead to intense anger and frustration.

5. Use assertiveness skills (covered in Module 7) if needed.

6. Reward yourself for managing these feelings.

Home Practice

Assignments in this section may include one or more of the following:

✐ Have the client complete the Tension Diary in the workbook.

✐ Have the client practice the relaxation exercise on a regular basis and record on the Relaxation Practice Log in the workbook.

✐ Have the client complete the A-B-C Form in the workbook.

✐ Have the client complete the A-B-C (STOP) D Form in the workbook.

Chapter 9 *Module 6: Communication Tools*

(Corresponds to chapter 6 of the workbook)

(3–4 Sessions)

Overview

Generally, it takes at least 3–4 sessions to learn these skills. Role playing and processing of the role-plays takes time, and the home practice
assigned often takes several weeks before results are observed. Thus, this
can be a very appropriate component for the Middle Phase of treatment,
when you are focusing on skill development.

This module focuses on teaching skills designed to improve communication between clients and their significant others. Often with older
adults, we find that either they are frequently in conflict with their significant others or they are estranged from them and wish they could
have more contact. Often that "distance" is rooted in long-term dis-
agreements and stress (e.g., the 70-year-old mother who disapproved
of her son's marriage 30 or 40 years ago and has had problems relating
to the daughter-in-law and their subsequent children. Now, she realizes
how cut off she has been from their lives and the lives of her grandchildren and would like to remedy this). This module would be appropriate
for such clients. It can also be useful for depressed and/or anxious older
individuals who do not have any close living family, or who have been
"loners" all their lives and now are recognizing that the lack of significant interpersonal relationships is a problem that they want to address
in therapy.

As with other advanced skills in this manual, teaching more effective
communication relies on the client knowing the basics of CBT. Typically, those segments are covered first, and this module is used after these
skills have been acquired. However, this module can also be effective
with clients who do not seem to be able to learn the basics effectively.

For such clients, learning by doing, through role playing and the like, can be a very effective way to teach the basic skills. Recognizing the impact of one's words at least (if not one's thoughts, directly) on others and changing the way of presenting oneself in order to achieve a particular goal requires both thinking and behaving differently and can be a very effective way for the client to improve communication skills.

EFFECTIVE COMMUNICATION

Materials Needed

- Copy of client workbook
- Whiteboard or easel

Outline

- Set the agenda
- Review home practice
- Introduce the communication continuum
- Discuss passive communication
- Discuss aggressive communication
- Discuss effective communication
- Introduce steps for communicating more effectively in conflict situations
- Summarize session
- Give mutual feedback
- Assign home practice

Learning to do this starts with teaching the older adult about the "communication continuum," which is a critical first step for older adults who are estranged from, or are in active conflict with, their significant others. Other approaches are recommended for those who have very limited interpersonal contacts and who wish to develop friendships and reach out to other people; this will be covered later in this module.

Effectively handling conflict with other family members or long-term friends can be a challenging skill to learn because speaking up for one's needs is difficult when one feels depressed or anxious. Older people, who are depressed and anxious, may not have the energy to talk to others about their emotional needs or they may not believe that they themselves are worthy enough to get these needs met by other people. It is also often very difficult to change highly overlearned patterns of relating to long-standing acquaintances or relatives. Being interpersonally effective requires a set of skills that clients may have, but not be able to use well in situations where there is emotional conflict and/or a history of misunderstandings.

First, explain to clients that there are different *styles* of communication that exist across a continuum. What style of communication one adopts often varies from person to person (e.g., with the client's spouse she may tend to communicate in one way, whereas with business associates or friends outside the home, the client's typical style may be different). You want to help clients understand this and help them focus on the style or manner of interacting that is giving them the most trouble in the present.

The central dimension of the continuum is the degree of respect one has for one's own personal rights and for the rights of the other person with whom one is in conflict or disagreement. The communication continuum has three key anchors: passive, effective or assertive, and aggressive. Refer to Figure 9.1 on the next page.

Below each label on this continuum is the description of the consequences of selecting that style. Being passive means that one's own personal rights and feelings are dismissed in favor of the rights and feelings of the other person. Being aggressive means that one's own

Passive	Effective (Assertive)	Aggressive
Your rights & feelings vs. others'	Your rights & feelings vs. others'	Your rights & feelings vs. others'
You Lose—They Win!	You Win—They Win!	You Win—They Lose!
(They dominate the interaction)	(A more equal exchange occurs)	(You dominate the interaction)

Figure 9.1

The Communication Continuum

personal rights are valued higher than those of the other person, who may ultimately feel dominated or humiliated by the communication. Communicating effectively generally means that both parties feel satisfied and valued in the interaction. Discuss the specifics of each style as follows.

Therapist Note

■ *Effective communication is sometimes referred to as "assertive," but use of this term is not necessary to get the point across, and not recommended with older adults who often disagree with its use. That engenders a side-bar discussion that is away from the focus of treatment and takes up valuable therapy time.* ■

Passive Communication

When we communicate passively, we are not expressing our feelings and our thoughts honestly. Communicating passively means that we speak in an apologetic manner that results in others disregarding us or putting down our statements. Passive communication also shows a lack of respect for other's abilities to handle problems. In general, the goal of passive communication is to please others while avoiding conflict. This style is often seen in long-married couples where one partner is more dominant (typically the male). For many older depressed women, learning to "speak up" in their marriage and be "heard" by their husbands is a goal of treatment. Likewise, they may want to learn to "speak up" appropriately in interactions with their adult children, who may not, for example, be saving for the grandchildren's education well enough. These interpersonal conflicts can reinforce depression by increasing the client's sense of low self-worth and being of low value to significant others.

You may want to use the case example of Lily in the workbook to demonstrate passive communication. The following questions can be used to discuss the case example.

1. *How do Lily's responses fail to show respect for her rights and possibly for her daughter's rights and feelings?*

2. *What might be some possible outcomes for Lily? Consider what her thoughts and her feelings are, and how this situation has already had several negative consequences both cognitively and behaviorally.*

3. *What kind of message do you think Lily's passive communication style gives her daughter? What about the negative impact on the grandchildren? Assess the "damage" to everyone concerned if Lily doesn't develop a more effective way to communicate with the harried, hassled daughter.*

Passive Communication Exercise

Ask the client to consider the last time she acted passively. Have the client complete a UTD for this situation to learn about her thoughts and feelings. Then, have the client look over the UTD to determine the costs and benefits of passive communication. Discuss what passive communication means to the client, and whether or not this is a pattern she wishes to continue. The "cost–benefit" analysis is very important to help the client see that the costs outweigh the benefits: If not short term, then clearly in the long term. Using the example of Lily can help to bring this "down to earth" and encourage the client to come up with her own stressful interpersonal interaction (or a series of them) to discuss.

Aggressive communication involves making statements that usually disregard the rights of others. The goal of aggressive communication is to dominate others and get them to do what you want. It is basically telling people, "This is what I want, and what you want is not as important to me."

You may want to use the case example of Lily in the workbook to demonstrate aggressive communication. The following questions can be used to discuss the case example:

1. *How does Lily's response fail to show respect for her daughter's rights and feelings?*

2. *What might be some possible outcomes for Lily and Marcia, besides the ones mentioned in the case example? Think long term: Continuing to have little or no contact with her granddaughters in the years ahead would be extremely difficult for this client. Therefore, it makes sense to try to work out a compromise so that the contact can be reinstated, and Marcia can feel less threatened by her mother's presence and ways of doing things (which reflect on Marcia, who may well be wondering if SHE'S a good mother). Consider what Marcia's thoughts and feelings might be.*

3. *What kind of message do you think Lily's aggressive communication style gives her family?* (You can point out that it is probably not good for the grandchildren to have zero contact with their grandmother, and this could be a positive learning experience for everyone if Lily would "make the first move" and try a different way of communicating with Marcia.)

It is important not to promise the client that the other person's response will actually change since it may not happen that way. The message the client needs to learn is that aggressive communication is not effective; in fact, it often results in the opposite outcome from what she wants.

Aggressive Communication Exercise

Ask the client to consider the last time she acted aggressively. It does not have to be the same kind of situation as reported here, but it should be a situation that is meaningful to the client. Have the client complete a UTD for this situation to learn about her thoughts and feelings. Then, have the client look over the UTD to determine the costs and benefits of aggressive communication. Discuss what aggressive communication means to the client and whether or not this is a pattern she wishes to continue. The "cost–benefit" analysis is very important to help the client see that the costs outweigh the benefits: If not in the short term, then clearly in the long term.

Effective Communication

In contrast to these two styles, communicating effectively involves expressing oneself clearly and honestly while considering both one's personal rights and feelings and the rights and feelings of others. Effective, expressive statements are those communications that are done without humiliating, dominating, or insulting the other person. This is not as easy as it sounds, since the other person in the interaction may "hear" or interpret what one is saying differently from what one's meaning is. Therefore, it is helpful to *practice effective communication* in the session, using several kinds of role-playing (to be described later in the chapter). This can help the client see the impact of her words on the other person. It can also help her develop alternative responses, which often will lead to a more positive outcome.

You may want to use the case example of Lily in the workbook to demonstrate a communication style that is likely to be more effective in reaching the desired goal. The following questions can be used to discuss the case example.

1. *How does Lily's response show respect for her rights and feelings as well as her daughter's?*

2. *What might be some possible outcomes in this situation (both positive and negative)? Consider what Lily's thoughts, feelings, and behaviors might be.*

3. *What kind of message do you think Lily's effective communication style gives Lily's daughter?*

4. *What kind of communication techniques, and role-play exercises, do you think would help the client to engage in, in session, in order to practice effective communication?*

It is up to the therapist to respond to this last question and to be thinking ahead to the next step, which is behavioral in nature. You will need to select which techniques to use now (in session) so that the client has the opportunity to practice new ways to communicate. This question is included here to stimulate the client's thinking along these lines as well. We have found it can be very productive to ask clients to think about what they want to learn. That may trigger some behavioral exercises that you have not thought of, up to this point.

Preparing the client for both a positive and a negative outcome is essential as we do not have control over the other person's responses. In our experience, "repairing" conflicted relationships like Lily and Marcia's takes time and effort. Often, the first attempt is rebuffed, and so the client needs to be prepared for this, and encouraged to try again, which she will want to do anyway, if it is really important. However, as this is an important situation in terms of maintaining, and sometimes worsening, the client's state of depression, it needs to be rehearsed carefully and alternative scenarios practiced. This emphasis on role playing is in addition to working on the thought record, both go hand in hand to bring about change.

Effective Communication Exercise

Ask the client to consider the last time she believes she communicated effectively with someone:

This can be an example from another domain of the client's life, such as work, or it can be an example from a time when the client communicated effectively with the person with whom she is now in conflict. The latter can have more "educational value," since it gives the therapist a better idea of how the other person actually responds in real-life situations when conflict is minimal, so you should try to obtain such an example if possible.

Have the client complete a UTD to learn about her thoughts and feelings about being able to communicate in a way that was effective and reasonable for both parties. Then, have the client look over her UTD to determine some of the costs and benefits of communicating in a manner that respects both parties' feelings and needs and that leads to a successful resolution. Discuss the behavioral outcomes from the interaction: if positive, they will be self-reinforcing. Continue again with discussion of Lily (see case example material in the workbook).

Steps in Deciding to Communicate More Effectively in Conflict Situations

Sum up this section by encouraging clients to consider the following issues before they are going to have an interpersonal interaction with someone with whom they are, or have been, in conflict:

1. What is the goal or objective of your message?

2. How might alternative methods of communication help you reach your goal?

3. Pick the communication style that will most likely provide the best outcome.

Home Practice

Assignments in this section may include one or more of the following:

✎ Have the client review the case example and record answers to the questions in the workbook.

✎ Have the client complete UTDs for passive, aggressive, and effective communication and consider costs and benefits of each style.

ROLE PLAYS

Materials Needed

- Copy of client workbook
- Whiteboard or easel

Outline

- Set the agenda
- Review home practice
- Introduce steps in deciding to communicate more effectively in conflicted situations
- Conduct first role play
- Conduct second role play
- Conduct third role play
- Continue with role plays as needed
- Summarize session
- Give mutual feedback
- Assign home practice

Role Playing

Role plays can be used in many different ways to help the client. For example, the therapist can take on the role of a person in the client's life with whom there is current conflict and try to simulate an exchange that might stimulate the development of alternative thoughts and actions by the client. Roles can be reversed, and the client can play the other person, while the therapist plays the client, thereby being a model and helping her experience how a different style of interaction might work.

Switching roles again (the client plays self) so that the client can practice using a new style of interacting with the problematic person can be extremely beneficial. The more often this exercise is repeated, the more likely the client will be effective in changing their interactive pattern with specific individuals. This technique is discussed in greater detail in later sections.

Therapist Note

■ *This 3-part role-play series is a good way to teach older adults how to communicate more effectively. To set the stage, a particular interpersonal situation needs to be delineated that is causing the client stress and that can be described in some detail to the therapist (so that the therapist can "get into the role"). Role-play segments should not be long and detailed, else they may become too stressful to foster new learning and change. Processing feelings and thoughts of the client after each role-play segment is extremely important in helping the client get a better perspective on how to change their "habitual" interactive pattern used in problematic relationships. Further practice usually strengthens its effectiveness. According to Wright, Basco, and Thase (2006), however, role playing is used less frequently than other techniques, because it can be more challenging for both the therapist and the client. Therapists must be sensitive to the possibility that for some clients this technique may be too challenging. In our experience, we have found this technique to be effective with many older clients who are experiencing conflictual relationships with significant others.* ■

3-Part Role Play: Part 1

We have included an example of a 3-part role play involving Harold as an illustration of how this technique works. This example is also presented in the client workbook. The therapist has the option of simply discussing this example with the client or using it as a model for practice prior to working directly with a personal conflictual relationship. The client's personal conflict can be a relationship that existed in the past or a relationship that is currently ongoing. In part 1, the client plays himself, while the therapist plays the other person in the interaction. Following is the case of Harold:

■ *Harold is a 70-year-old retired teacher who became depressed subsequent to his retirement 3 years ago from a full-time college teaching position. He was advised to retire when he was "at the top of his game" but he had not anticipated how lonely and bored he would be, without regular contact with students, a regular schedule, and purpose and meaning for his life. Therefore, he began contacting his former department chairperson to ask for his old job back. He describes that his last encounter with his former boss was very stressful and unsuccessful: He tried to explain why he needed his old job back and felt he was not heard, was "brushed off" by the department chairman, and was doomed to failure. In the first role play, the client asks for his job back, and the therapist plays the department chairperson.* ■

Enacting the situation as closely as possible to what the client described actually happened helps both individuals become aware of thoughts, feelings, and actions that probably occurred and sets the stage for the next 2 parts of the role play. The role play should go on no more than 5 min or so, with about 10 additional minutes spent processing the feelings and thoughts that the client is aware of.

3-Part Role Play: Part 2

Next, the client plays the other person (in this case, the department chairperson), and the therapist plays the client. But here the therapist plays the client *communicating effectively*. Continuing with the case example:

■ *Instead of demanding his old job back, the therapist could explore alternatives with the chairperson such as a part-time or volunteer position. The client meanwhile (as the chairperson) can develop a greater empathy for being in that other person's shoes. Typically, they become aware of concerns the other person may have that they were not aware of before. For example, the chairperson may not have the budget or the authority to hire a full-time person, no matter who they are. He/she may also be concerned that in the 3 years of retirement, the client has "fallen behind" in his field and would not have the most up-to-date information to teach the students.* ■

If the client can express 1 or 2 of these concerns, she will develop some empathy for the chairperson's position, which can make it easier to discuss things in a rational, nonthreatening, not overly emotional manner. It is also helpful to ask the client to predict how the interaction is going to go, before doing the second role play; this usually produces a spate of negative thoughts that can be challenged before or after the second role play, with the object being to help the client realize that negative expectations for the interaction can lead to self-fulfilling prophecies. On the other hand, by encouraging a positive problem-solving attitude, you can empower the client. If she grasps that even briefly, she will want more time to practice!

After the 5 min second role play, again there's about 10 min spent processing the client's thoughts and feelings. Often at this time, the client is developing more of an awareness of how she was coming across, and how that could be improved upon. Presumably, the therapist has been able to role model more effective communication in this segment, thereby showing the client some alternatives ways that, presumably, turn out better than in the first interaction.

3-Part Role Play: Part 3

In the third part of the role play, the client again plays himself, and the therapist again plays the other person. In this exchange, the client is encouraged to practice other ways of making the request so that the client has the chance to develop options and to try them out, in a safe environment, with a "coach" right there to give feedback. Usually, this is a more successful experience than the first role play was, and that contrast is in itself informative.

After about 5 min again of role play, another 10 min or so are spent processing what was said, how it felt, what the thoughts were that were associated with it, and what the resultant feelings were. Generally, by now, the client has had the chance to practice, literally, different ways of making the request, and can learn from the role play how these different ways of presenting the request may be received by the other person. Continuing with the case example of Harold:

> ▪ *In the long run, Harold did not get his old job back; he did, however, assume a volunteer spot with considerable responsibility. This helped the college that was experiencing a budget crisis, gave him a reason to get up in the morning, made him feel useful and needed, and improved his mood. The client credited his eventual success with the practice role plays, since he truly was too depressed, and desperate, to be thinking of "effective" ways to communicate: he was aware mainly of his needs and not of the total situation or context within which they would be (or not be) addressed.* ▪

Home Practice and Continued Role Play

For the client to get the most out of this exercise, the therapist needs to be prepared with some alternative responses (so that he/she can model them) and timing needs to be monitored so that the entire process can be completed in one full session. Generally, this leads to the home practice assignment of actually talking with the identified person and then reporting back next time how it went. Whether or not to make this the assignment depends on the judgment of the clinician: If he or she thinks the client is ready for the interaction and will in fact be able to implement what was learned, AND if there appears to be a reasonable chance for success, then it is an excellent assignment. Whether or not the client gets what she wants, she will learn something from the experience. However, if the clinician thinks that there is a high probability of failure, or if the client did not really seem to understand how to proceed, then it is not advisable. Home practice then could be to select a less challenging or less emotional situation, and practice effective communication in that situation.

For some clients, role playing is very effective: They are able to "get into it" and they learn through modeling, practice, and feedback. For others, it is extremely difficult to get them to participate. In those cases, it is not worth struggling with clients to get them to do this. If they are reluctant, then it is necessary to find other ways to help them restructure their interpersonal interactions so that they are more effective.

Home Practice

Assignments in this section may include one or more of the following:

 Carry out home practice assignments as discussed in session.

Review materials in workbook, and identify other difficult interpersonal interactions to discuss and practice in the next session.

OTHER WAYS TO BECOME INTERPERSONALLY EFFECTIVE

Materials Needed

- Copy of client workbook

- Whiteboard or easel

Outline

- Set the agenda

- Review home practice

- Recommend the use of "I" statements

- Discuss the importance of compromise

- Teach the client the "broken record" technique

- Teach the client how to communicate effectively when developing new relationships

- Summarize session

- Give mutual feedback

- Assign home practice

Besides learning through role-plays, there are other specific techniques that the clinician can teach clients in order to help them enhance their ability to communicate effectively. Here are some techniques that we have found effective with older adults:

Using "I" Statements

Using "I" statements (instead of "you" did this and that and it's "your fault" or "you should do X or Y") helps to ground the person in the interaction, and helps to clarify what it is that she is really seeking from the interaction. For example, if a 90-year-old widowed woman living alone says "why don't you come over more to visit" to her adult children, she is not likely to get many visitors. That kind of statement tends to make the other person defensive or may sound accusatory. Instead, she could state clearly: "Mary Jo and Marlene, I would like you come to visit me more. I am lonely and I miss spending time with you. Can we figure out a day and time when you can drop by and spend an hour with me?"—this is a definite invitation, instead of a vague demand, and so is more likely to result in a positive response. Again, stating clearly what one wants or needs is an integral part of communicating effectively.

Compromise

Another technique is learning "the art of negotiation and how to compromise" or "developing options if I can't get exactly what I want." This is a very good intervention for those whose thinking tends to run in "all or none" terms. Such clients seem to think that if they can't have it all, then why bother? Explain that placing that kind of interpersonal demand on other people usually does not result in their going along with the client; more often, they tend to back away, since the demand is too extreme. Consider the following case example:

■ *Mary is a 68-year-old caregiver for her husband with dementia. She wants to take some time off from caregiving to get needed dental surgery done, but she has difficulty getting a reliable person to come in and "sit" with her husband while she is out. She would like to have a whole day off, but the caregiver who was recommended by a neighbor can only work 4 h/day for her. If Mary argues with this person to try and convince her to*

*stay for 8 h instead of 4, she is very likely to lose her completely. On the
other hand, being willing to negotiate how many hours can really be
arranged for the caregiver to come and take over will lead to a "win–win"
situation in which the care-recipient is being supervised while the caregiver
can do some things for herself that she had been putting off. Alternatively, if
she kept insisting on the full day of respite, she could wind up with nothing
of what she wants. The therapist can challenge this "all or none" thinking
by referring back to the earlier chapters in this manual and reviewing the
cognitive skills, such as cost–benefit analysis, that can be brought into
play here.* ▪

This example also illustrates how several distinct components of CBT
can be brought to bear on a particular situation. The more clients can
see the interconnectedness of the CBT strategies, the more deeply they
are processing this new information, and the more likely they are to
retain it and to use it in their everyday lives.

The Broken Record Technique

Sometimes negotiation is not possible. The broken record technique is
a method where one straightforward statement is repeated. This technique keeps the goal clearly in mind while being respectful of one's own
needs and, to a lesser extent, the needs of the other person in the interaction. This technique is particularly effective when dealing with obstinate
people who may be pressuring the client to do something she would
rather avoid. This technique is also helpful in communicating with
Alzheimer's patients or post-stroke patients who quickly forget information. Finally, it can be a useful way for the client to get something
that she wants, depending on the other person's willingness to respond.

Case Example: Jillian's Use of the Broken Record Technique

You may want to use the following case example to illustrate how to use
the broken record technique:

▪ *Jillian's daughter often asks her to take care of her granddaughter
without advance notice, even though she may have plans to do something*

else. Jillian feels that her daughter takes advantage of her and has little concern for her welfare. On one particular day, Jillian had made plans with her friends to go on a day trip that she had been looking forward to for a long time. On the morning of Jillian's plans, her daughter calls and asks for help. Jillian clearly demonstrates her concern for her daughter's dilemma, but she is not willing to change her long-awaited plans with her friends. She uses the broken record technique in her communication. Their conversation goes as follows:

Daughter: Mom, I need to get my car repaired, can Susie spend the afternoon with you?

Jillian: I have plans today, and I will not be able to watch her for you today.

Daughter: Where are you going? Maybe I can meet you? It's just for the afternoon.

Jillian: I'm sorry, I will not be able to do it. I have plans. Perhaps, we could do this tomorrow.

Daughter: Why not? I'm stuck. I need to get the car repaired, and I have no one else to ask to watch Susie.

Jillian: I can see that you are in a bind. I'm so sorry, but I have plans that I really can't change at this point. If you can put off getting your car repaired till tomorrow, I'll be glad to watch Susie. ■

The following questions can be used to discuss the case example; space to answer is provided in the workbook.

1.   What was the major point that Jillian conveyed? How do you feel about how she went about it?

2.   What was Jillian's goal?

3.   Do you think she was successful in reaching her goal?

4.   Can you think of how and when you might use the "broken record" technique in your interactions?

Ask the client to imagine a situation when using the broken record technique would be appropriate to use and describe it to you.

Therapist Note

■ *It is not a good idea to just briefly discuss the technique and then tell the client to practice or to use it for home practice. It is more effective to do a role play focusing on this particular technique so that clients develop some sense of confidence and mastery before trying to employ it in their daily lives.* ■

The "broken record" is a very effective technique for saying "no." It also provides a framework for how to ask for things that are needed: asking repeatedly, in a calm manner, and "sticking to your guns" (assuming the request is reasonable).

Summary of Steps Involved in Using the Broken Record Technique

Summarize the steps for the client as follows.

1. Stick to one point and don't get sidetracked.

2. Show respect for the other person. The goal statement can be preceded with a supportive comment.

3. Repeat the goal statement with *minor* modifications.

4. Avoid explanations for the chosen statement. This is not necessary. Explanations will introduce negotiation to the conversation. When this happens, the focus of the goal is often lost.

Therapist Note

■ *An important feature of the broken record and other techniques used to handle conflicted interactions is that it keeps the client in a "strategic" mode of communication. This helps them avoid becoming emotional, which most often results in counterproductive communications. Once clients experience success in using such strategies, it encourages them to be more "observant" of what is really transpiring in the communication. We refer to it as "going to the meta-level" or "above" oneself to observe the content and the impact of the interaction. Older clients often report that this helps keep them from getting angry or becoming anxious and depressed.* ■

This section is for the client who is alone and wants to reach out to people, knows she needs to do this for her mental health (realizes the importance of social support, etc.), but doesn't have the skills for initiating and carrying on conversations with people who are not family members. This is a different kind of problem faced by many depressed older adults than what we have been discussing thus far in this section. Due to loss of spouse or partner, friends dying or moving away, and changes in health that may preclude their continuing to do hobbies that provided them with a social network (e.g., golf, tennis, and bridge club), many older adults find that their social networks have shrunk considerably. Often, this is a gradual process that takes place over a number of years and may not even be noticed until it has gotten to rather extreme proportions. Role playing can be used as part of a skill set to increase the likelihood that a person who is interpersonally isolated will begin to reach out to other people and begin to develop satisfying personal relationships.

■ *Richard is a 78-year-old retired software engineer whose wife died after a prolonged illness about 5 years ago. Although he is intellectually active and uses his home computer daily to remain in contact with the "tech world," he has gradually disengaged from friendships associated with work. For example, there are periodic reunions for former employees as well as several company events each year that he is invited to, but he begs off, saying he does not want to go alone, and he won't know anyone when he's there. A lot of his old friends have died or moved away or are too physically ill to attend. Richard has a son who lives nearby, and there are four grandchildren with whom he has contact: He helps to babysit the grandchildren and has dinner often with his son's family. He reports these to be pleasant events that he looks forward to eagerly. In the course of describing these relationships, he contrasted the time he spends with them (which is enjoyable) with the time he spends alone (which is most of the day and which he described as "empty"). This brought the issue to light and after some discussion of its importance, it became a focus for therapy.*

There are no interpersonal conflicts with the family; but Richard reports severe bouts of loneliness that he believes maintain his depression. He has gotten to the point that he does not want to go out of the house except to go to his son's and to keep his doctor's appointments. He laments about this, but despite support and encouragement from his family to attend a senior center, he has not done so. The therapist decided that Richard needed some skill building in the area of how to form friendships: How to meet and talk with strangers, how to set up lunch appointments, how to explore if the other person seemed interested in developing a friendship, and similar skills. Richard agreed that, strange as it sounded (he is a highly educated man, after all, with a very successful career history), he did not know how to initiate conversation with someone he'd just met. He was extremely anxious about even going to the senior center and so the situation had to be addressed on several levels. ■

First, small goals had to be established, in a hierarchical fashion, so that he would achieve some success each time that would encourage him to continue (e.g., driving to the senior center, going in to pick up a schedule; taking a tour of the facility; all of these things were done before any home practice assignment was given to go there for lunch and sit down beside someone and talk with the person).

Second, relaxation exercises were taught to reduce his anxiety: He was able to learn how to take slow, deep breaths and this seemed to calm him.

Third, role playing was done in session to help him practice what to say (and what not to say) to a stranger he'd just met. He realized he could discuss current events since he reads a newspaper every day and keeps up on what is happening in the world. He decided he could read one or two books on the bestseller list and make notes about who the characters were and what the plot was (so he would not forget the details), since many people like to discuss the books they read. He is an enthusiastic computer buff and was able to talk about some technical subjects in the role plays, thinking he might run across another older person like himself who had done similar work in the past.

■ *Armed with these topics noted above and having practiced what to say for the better part of two full sessions, Richard felt confident to actually go to lunch at the senior center and talk with the person next to him. This was successfully accomplished after two attempts; the first time, he was too anxious to eat and he left early. The second time, he did the relaxation exercise before he entered the building and he said this gave him a sense of control and so he was able to follow through as planned. Subsequent therapy sessions focused on "next steps"—after you meet someone interesting to talk with, how do you invite them to lunch? Or to a movie? Or to do something else together? It took two additional sessions to work on these issues; again, role playing was done, focusing on "less effective" compared to "more effective" ways to do these things. Richard was fully engaged in this process and was able to take what he learned in the office into the senior center. He is now attending on average 3 days per week and is slowly expanding his social network. He has thought about returning to church services as well (something he had not done since his wife's death). He believes he will find acceptance there and people to talk with, so this is likely to be his next step in the process of developing a meaningful social network.* ■

Other clients may be too depressed to focus on a goal such as this, which is ambitious and does require considerable energy to implement. However, even if the client is not able to go beyond the family for interpersonal satisfaction and support, she can surely improve those relationships. We therefore routinely advise therapists working with older adults to be aware of the salience of these issues (loneliness and social isolation), and when appropriate, to incorporate techniques such as these into their therapeutic work.

Remember, if clients are having trouble initiating effective methods of communication, encourage the use of a UTD to help them understand what thoughts are blocking their use of appropriate techniques.

Home Practice

Assignments in this section may include one or more of the following:

✎ Have the client practice effective communication and try specific techniques, such as using "I" statements, compromise, or the broken record technique.

✎ Encourage the client to take steps to develop new relationships as needed (e.g., talking for 5 min to a stranger at the senior center and reporting back to you how it went, and whether or not it was as difficult to do as the client feared).

Late Phase of Therapy

Introduction

The primary focus of the late phase of therapy is the preparation for termination. This usually requires 3–4 sessions, and it is recommended to space the last few sessions out (e.g., biweekly rather than weekly). Termination of the relationship with the therapist can be stressful for any client. It may be particularly difficult for older clients who have few friends and family members or who report that loneliness is one of their primary target complaints. The therapist often becomes an important person in the client's life who provides some companionship. Increasing time between sessions at the very end of therapy can help the client adjust to this loss. It also gives clients an opportunity to try skills they have learned on their own. Clients can observe whether or not they are now able to deal effectively with stressful situations without immediate consultation. When a client returns for a spaced session, the therapist and the client can then decide together what changes may be required, if any, to help the client maintain the gains made during therapy. A booster session roughly 6 months after termination to evaluate progress and make any necessary adjustments in the skills being used can also be helpful in minimizing relapse.

Maintenance Guide and Continued Use of Skills

This phase begins with a review of the skills or techniques the client has learned for dealing with stressful situations, and of these, which seemed to work best, and what might be possible explanations for why this is the case. We recommend that the therapist introduce at the start of this phase the idea of developing a "maintenance guide," which the client can complete over the next couple of sessions with the help of the therapist. A format for completing a maintenance guide is included at the end of the workbook, and an example of a completed guide is included in Chapter 7 of the workbook.

Recent research has documented that clients who continue to use the skills they learned during a 2-year follow-up are much less likely to experience a high level of depressive symptoms (Powers, Thompson, & Gallagher-Thompson, 2008). While causality is not demonstrated in these results, it would seem to make sense to encourage clients to use their workbooks and continue to apply the skills they have learned. Furthermore, the helpfulness level of skills used was more highly correlated with the level of symptoms than with the frequency of skill usage. This suggests that during the late phase of therapy, it would be important to determine which skills are most helpful to the client and to set up explicit guidelines detailing when and how these should be applied. During booster sessions, in particular, the therapist should work with the client to determine the helpfulness level of specific skills and encourage or dissuade their continued use accordingly.

Disengagement From the Therapist

Another important issue to discuss early in the late phase is the loss of the relationship with the therapist. As noted earlier, termination is often stressful. Clients may become anxious and experience thoughts that they won't be able to make adjustments without the therapist's help. It then becomes important to clarify to clients that they are ultimately responsible for their mastery of the skills. Clients need to make attributions that they are the agents of behavioral and emotional change as opposed to the therapist. The successful client will have the belief that "I can do this on my own." This facilitates the development of high self-esteem and self-efficacy, which are important contributors to a client's ability to use her new skills at times of imminent distress.

It is useful to reflect back on earlier sessions and identify what strategies seemed to work best for the individual client. In this phase more than others, maintain the basic elements but keep assignments as simple and concrete as possible, with an emphasis on tailoring them to client needs. It's critical to help clients appreciate and use their own abilities to cope with losses and negative changes. An important step in this process is understanding how they have coped in the past. Incorporating more formal "life review" techniques into the therapy as you approach termination can help the client evaluate her life in as positive and fulfilling vein as possible. If this by chance leads to negative recollections, then using the UTD can often help the client identify distortions and counteract them with rational reconstructions. Themes such as "coming to terms with the meaning of one's life" may also emerge at this point, and helping the client develop highly specific and structured strategies for dealing with these issues can be helpful.

In these final sessions we recommend that consideration be given to referring clients to appropriate community resources, to help them continue to get needed support. For example, encouraging them to find local "support groups" for coping with chronic illness can promote continued well-being long after formal therapy is over. In addition, a list of national resources is included in the Appendix and may be of relevance to some clients at this point in the process.

Chapter 10 | *Module 7: Termination*

(Corresponds to chapter 7 of the workbook)

(3–4 Sessions)

Materials Needed

- Copy of client workbook

- Whiteboard or easel

- 6-column UTD form

- How Will I Handle Stressful Situations in the Future? form

- Danger Signals form

- Maintenance Guide template

Outline

- Set the agenda

- Review home practice

- Schedule the ending process

- Process termination issues

- Discuss maintaining changes after therapy ends

- Review skills learned in therapy

- Plan for future stressful situations

- Identify danger signals and make a plan for dealing with them

- Discuss how to use the workbook as a resource

- Summarize session

- Give mutual feedback

- Assign home practice

Overview

The final 3–4 sessions should be devoted to termination and maintenance issues. This involves the same components that need to be incorporated into the basic structure of each session: (a) set an agenda; (b) review home practice; (c) select at least one topic to work on in depth; (d) summarize; (e) set up new home practice assignment; and (f) do mutual feedback.

But note that the focus of these sessions will be on termination itself – no new topics/problem areas should be introduced at this time. To do so may interfere with planned termination, although if a major new problem arises at this time, it may be necessary to re-negotiate for several additional sessions before getting into this final phase of the work.

Scheduling the Ending Process

We recommend that therapy end in a gradual and systematic way. The final few sessions could be spaced out (i.e., instead of held weekly, perhaps biweekly) to give the client time to disengage from the therapeutic relationship and to use the tools learned in therapy independently to deal with stressful events and negative moods. We have found that more gradual terminations are easier for the client to adjust to and are associated with increased long-term improvement. We also recommend, if needed, the possibility of scheduling "booster sessions" after the last formal session. Booster sessions are designed as a "check-in" to see how the client is using these skills on his own. We often schedule booster sessions to occur anywhere from 3 to 6 months after the official last session.

During the final sessions, encourage discussions about the following:

- what ending therapy means to the client

- the client's ideas about what was more helpful and what was less helpful during treatment

- the client's feelings about his relationship with you (the therapist)

Talking directly about these issues helps create a more positive ending and will give the client a sense of closure that is very important. Ask the client to come prepared to talk about these things; he may, perhaps, want to write out some notes on these topics. You can also encourage the client to complete UTDs related to his fears and concerns about ending therapy.

Other topics that may come up at this point in time are whether or not the client should continue with another professional therapist, go on antidepressant medication, or perhaps join a self-help group or a support group of some kind.

Therapist Note

■ *These are all important issues that should be talked about frankly and thoroughly at this time. Remember there are no general guidelines that are appropriate for all clients. Individual people have individual needs.* ■

Maintaining Changes After Therapy Has Ended

The Maintenance Guide is a specific document created by both you and the client that consolidates the client's experience in therapy; it is used to review skills and prepare for possible problems in the future. We recommend creating this guide over 3 sessions before the final "goodbye" session. This guide can be started in session and the client can complete or add to it for home practice.

Use of UTDs

Also, for those clients who use UTDs well, it can be very helpful to review copies of actual UTDs completed during treatment. This review can be used to see what were some important issues in the beginning of therapy and what was the progression over time in the client's understanding of the problems and reduction of depression and other negative effects associated with the problems. The client may photocopy blank UTDs from the workbook for future use.

Example of a Maintenance Guide

An example of a Maintenance Guide has been provided in the workbook. You may want to review the case example of John with the client to demonstrate how helpful the guide could be in the case a negative event or some crisis occurs that might trigger a depressive episode.

Review of Skills

To begin preparation for the maintenance guide, ask the client to review the skills he learned throughout therapy. The workbook includes space to list cognitive, behavioral, and interpersonal skills. Ask the client the following questions:

- "What were the cognitive skills you have learned?"

- "What were the behavioral skills you have learned?"

- "What were the interpersonal skills you have learned?"

- "What skills did you use to achieve your goals?"

Ask the client to think about the situations that are likely to arise in the future that may exacerbate symptoms and result in depression. Encourage him to list these on the form in the workbook (How Will I Handle Stressful Situations in the Future?). Discuss the following questions:

■ "What kinds of high-risk situations might you experience that would send your thoughts and emotions into a downward spiral?"

■ "How will you handle future stressful situations?"

Have the client think of specific cognitive, behavioral, and interpersonal skills (from his earlier list) that would help in each particular situation, and record these in the space provided on the form.

Rehearsal

Clients may also find it helpful to rehearse for future situations in session. Role plays can clarify how clients will handle specific situations and increase their confidence in their new skills. This is particularly important for clients who have functional impairments that will need to be compensated for with overlearning. An example of one such client follows:

■ *Helen, an 80-year-old female recently widowed, was confronted with the problem of completing and submitting her yearly income taxes. In past years, her husband always took care of this, and she had no idea about where to start or what to do. Helen was beginning to have some memory and word-finding problems as well, which was very stressful for her. Since childhood, she also had problems in doing arithmetic, which made her anxious, and she subsequently had avoided mathematics throughout her entire education. After collecting all the financial records in one place, she began to panic. A plethora of cognitive distortions were occurring, leading finally to the idea that she would be arrested and have to spend the rest of her life in jail. A year ago, this state of affairs would more than likely have precipitated a severe episode of depression. However, in this instance, her emotions triggered a sequence of responses she had practiced while in the last phase of therapy. Her first response, Rule Number One, was to say the word "stop" emphatically; "this problem can be solved." Rule Number*

Two—"Do a UTD immediately!" Rule Number Three—"Identify the distortions for what they are." Rule Number Four—"Say to yourself, there is a solution—I'll think better after I do my relaxation." Rule Number Five—"If nothing comes to mind, check my workbook." Rule Number Six—"Counteract the distortions." "Now I'm ready to do problem solving." The first important realization was, "I don't have to do this by myself. Everyone needs help with this. It doesn't mean I'm deteriorating." This led to the second step to get more information. Check with friends. Get a reliable tax consultant, etc. The fact that Helen and her therapist worked diligently to develop and overpractice this scenario made it readily available at a time of serious stress.

Recognizing and Planning for Danger Signals

Encourage the client to talk about "danger signals" that should serve as warning signs that low moods are again present and getting more severe. Let the client know that sometimes depressive reactions occur, despite our best efforts. For example, a person may become overwhelmed by one very big negative event (such as death of a loved one) or by a series of smaller but frequent negative events (several bad things happening at once, overtaxing one's ability to cope). Emphasize that this can happen to anyone.

Identifying Danger Signals

It is important that the client think back to this most recent bout of depression and try to remember what the main symptoms were. Help the client make a list of the symptoms that he would consider to be his danger signals (space is provided in the workbook). This way he can notice them right away when they happen and make immediate plans for constructive action. Discussing the client's prior history will help a great deal here. Questions to ask might include the following:

■ "Did you mainly have trouble eating, sleeping, or with your energy level?"

- "Were you mainly preoccupied with negative thoughts about yourself and the future?"

- "Were you primarily sad, angry, anxious, or perhaps lonely, in terms of mood?"

- "How did you function? What areas of your functioning seemed to be affected by your depression?"

Making a Plan

The final task is to develop a concrete plan for what to do if/when serious depressive symptoms resurface. Who can the client call? What should he do if you are no longer in the area, or are not available, and he needs therapy again? You should have specific answers to these questions, so that you can terminate with your client in confidence. A related issue is that of making referrals at this time to community resources (e.g., appropriate support groups) that are likely to be of benefit to clients to help them maintain their gains. This is, of course, an individual decision, but in our experience, helping clients to "hook up" to community-based services is often very helpful as they transition out of formal therapy. A listing of a wide variety of national resources is included in the appendix to give you direction and assistance in locating appropriate follow-up services. Since finances are often an issue for older clients, being able to provide them with specific information about free or low-cost services is usually very much appreciated. It also helps to ease the termination process and conveys the message that ongoing support is "out there" and may be worth considering to help with maintenance of gains.

The Workbook as a Resource

All the notes, exercises, and forms can be found in the workbook. Instruct the client to keep it in a place where it is easily found. Encourage the use of the workbook as a written record of the work done in therapy. Clients may find it helpful to review certain sections as needed.

Final assignments may include one or more of the following:

✎ Have the client fill out 6-column UTD forms if helpful.

✎ Have the client complete the How Will I Handle Stressful Situations in the Future? form.

✎ Have the client complete the Danger Signals form.

✎ Have the client complete the Maintenance Guide.

The California Older Person's Pleasant Events Schedule (COPPES)

Following the COPPES is information on how to administer and score the measure.

Contact information is listed in the "Feedback" section of the instructions.

Name: _____ Date: _____

This is a list of 66 events that people tend to find pleasant. For each event, make 2 ratings:

How *often* did this event happen to you in the past month?
   0 = Not at all
   1 = 1–6 times
   2 = 7 or more times

How *pleasant, enjoyable, or rewarding* was this event? If the event did not occur, then please rate how pleasant you think it would have been if it had occurred.
   0 = Was not or would not have been pleasant
   1 = Was or would have been somewhat pleasant
   2 = Was or would have been very pleasant

Here are two sample events with the answers properly filled in. Please remember to circle an answer for both HOW OFTEN and HOW PLEASANT for each event.

Please circle ONE number in EACH column for each item	HOW OFTEN in the past month? 0 = Not at all 1 = 1–6 times 2 = 7 or more times Circle ONE number	HOW PLEASANT was it or would it have been? 0 = Not pleasant 1 = Somewhat pleasant 2 = Very pleasant Circle ONE number
A. Winning the lottery	⓪ 1 2	0 1 ②
B. Writing a letter	0 ① 2	0 ① 2

Please circle ONE number in EACH column for each item	HOW OFTEN in the past month? 0 = Not at all 1 = 1–6 times 2 = 7 or more times Circle ONE number			HOW PLEASANT was it or would it have been? 0 = Not pleasant 1 = Somewhat pleasant 2 = Very pleasant Circle ONE number		
1. Looking at clouds	0	1	2	0	1	2
2. Being with friends	0	1	2	0	1	2
3. Having people show an interest in what I say	0	1	2	0	1	2
4. Thinking about pleasant memories	0	1	2	0	1	2
5. Shopping	0	1	2	0	1	2
6. Seeing beautiful scenery	0	1	2	0	1	2
7. Having a frank and open conversation	0	1	2	0	1	2
8. Doing a job well	0	1	2	0	1	2
9. Listening to sounds of nature	0	1	2	0	1	2
10. Having coffee, tea, etc., with friends	0	1	2	0	1	2
11. Thinking about myself	0	1	2	0	1	2
12. Being complimented or told I have done something well	0	1	2	0	1	2
13. Doing volunteer work	0	1	2	0	1	2
14. Planning trips or vacations	0	1	2	0	1	2
15. Kissing, touching, showing affection	0	1	2	0	1	2
16. Being praised by people I admire	0	1	2	0	1	2
17. Meditating	0	1	2	0	1	2
18. Listening to music	0	1	2	0	1	2

continued

19. Seeing good things happen to family or friends	0	1	2	0	1	2
20. Collecting recipes	0	1	2	0	1	2
21. Doing a project my own way	0	1	2	0	1	2
22. Seeing or smelling a flower or plant	0	1	2	0	1	2
23. Saying something clearly	0	1	2	0	1	2
24. Thinking about something good in the future	0	1	2	0	1	2
25. Looking at the stars or moon	0	1	2	0	1	2
26. Being told I am needed	0	1	2	0	1	2
27. Working on a community project	0	1	2	0	1	2
28. Complimenting or praising someone	0	1	2	0	1	2
29. Watching a sunset	0	1	2	0	1	2
30. Thinking about people I like	0	1	2	0	1	2
31. Completing a difficult task	0	1	2	0	1	2
32. Amusing people	0	1	2	0	1	2
33. Baking because I feel creative	0	1	2	0	1	2
34. Reading literature	0	1	2	0	1	2
35. Being with someone I love	0	1	2	0	1	2
36. Having an original idea	0	1	2	0	1	2
37. Having peace and quiet	0	1	2	0	1	2
38. Listening to the birds sing	0	1	2	0	1	2
39. Making a new friend	0	1	2	0	1	2

continued

40. Being asked for help or advice	O	I	2	O	I	2
41. Bargain hunting	O	I	2	O	I	2
42. Reading magazines	O	I	2	O	I	2
43. Feeling a divine presence	O	I	2	O	I	2
44. Expressing my love to someone	O	I	2	O	I	2
45. Giving advice to others based on past experience	O	I	2	O	I	2
46. Solving a problem, puzzle, crossword	O	I	2	O	I	2
47. Arranging flowers	O	I	2	O	I	2
48. Helping someone	O	I	2	O	I	2
49. Getting out of the city (to the mountains, seashore, desert)	O	I	2	O	I	2
50. Having spare time	O	I	2	O	I	2
51. Being needed	O	I	2	O	I	2
52. Meeting someone new of the same sex	O	I	2	O	I	2
53. Exploring new areas	O	I	2	O	I	2
54. Having a clean house	O	I	2	O	I	2
55. Doing creative crafts	O	I	2	O	I	2
56. Going to church	O	I	2	O	I	2
57. Being loved	O	I	2	O	I	2
58. Visiting a museum	O	I	2	O	I	2
59. Having a daily plan	O	I	2	O	I	2
60. Being with happy people	O	I	2	O	I	2

continued

61. Listening to classical music	0	1	2	0	1	2
62. Shopping for a new outfit	0	1	2	0	1	2
63. Taking inventory of my life	0	1	2	0	1	2
64. Planning or organizing something	0	1	2	0	1	2
65. Smiling at people	0	1	2	0	1	2
66. Being near sand, grass, a stream	0	1	2	0	1	2

Scoring Recommendations: Options for How Clinicians Can Use the COPPES in their CBT Practice

The California Older Person's Pleasant Events Schedule (COPPES) is the first self-report measure of its kind developed from a sample of approximately 600 older adults in northern California. It was designed to be used flexibly by the clinician to assist in the process of identifying pleasant events or activities that the client will increase as part of his CBT treatment. The COPPES has 66 items that describe different pleasant activities or situations, such as, "having coffee with a friend, listening to birds in nature or being complimented for doing a good job." These items can be considered individually or they can be grouped into several meaningful categories described later. Items are scored according to frequency of occurrence and also level of pleasure obtained when they occur. The practitioner can obtain useful information about a client's preferences for pleasant events by simple visual inspection of the scale or by obtaining means for each category and comparing those with data obtained from a normative sample. Categories within the scale can be scored manually or by a specially designed (free) software program. Means for the categories can be compared with a normative sample of elderly community volunteers. Instructions for administration and scoring will be explained in more detail in the sections that follow.

COPPES Instructions to be Reviewed With the Client

The client is asked to rate the FREQUENCY of occurrence (in the past month) of each item in the scale, and then the PLEASURE or ENJOYABILITY of each item. Even if the event did not occur during the month, the client is asked to rate the pleasure or enjoyment he thinks he would have experienced. It is important that the client understands this point so that responses can be correctly interpreted. If the client cannot complete the form without assistance (due to problems such as visual and/or coordination deficits) you can complete it in-session or ask the client to do it with a trusted family member.

The purpose of using the COPPES is to assist the client to generate his personal list of pleasant activities to track and to increase them, in order to gain more control over mood and to enhance positive affect. While one could simply ASK the client for a list of potentially pleasant events to be increased, and not use either of the methods described here, we have not found that to be very effective with depressed individuals who often cannot generate more than a couple such events. The use of a scale like the COPPES facilitates this process by asking them about a broad array of activities – some of which they may have done in the past but have abandoned when they became depressed; others that they just might want to try now, for whatever reason.

Understanding the DOMAINS/SUBSCALES of this Measure

As you review the measure, you will intuitively note that there are a number of sub-scales (ways of grouping the items) that tap different domains of enjoyability. It is not imperative to use these subscales in discussions with the client, but they are useful to consider if there is time to do these groupings. There are 5 subscales: Socializing, Relaxing, Contemplating, Being Effective, and Doing Things, and the 66 items can be clustered into one of these scales. The code for placing items into the subscales is as follows:

   I. Socializing: 8 Items
   (Item Number/Item)

15	Kissing, touching, showing affection
19	Seeing good things happen to family or friends
28	Complimenting or praising someone
35	Being with someone I love
39	Making a new friend
44	Expressing my love to someone
52	Meeting someone new of the same sex
65	Smiling at people

II. Relaxing: 12 items
(Item Number/Item)

6   Seeing beautiful scenery

9   Listening to sounds of nature

18   Listening to music

25   Looking at the stars or moon

29   Watching a sunset

34   Reading literature

38   Listening to the birds sing

49   Getting out of the city (to the mountains, seashore, desert)

53   Exploring new areas

58   Visiting a museum

61   Listening to classical music

66   Being near sand, grass, a stream

III. Contemplating: 9 items
(Item Number/Item)

4   Thinking about pleasant memories

11   Thinking about myself

17   Meditating

30   Thinking about people I like

37   Having peace and quiet

43   Feeling a divine presence

50   Having spare time

56   Going to church

63   Taking inventory of my life

IV. Being Effective: 9 Items
(Item Number/Item)

16   Being praised by people I admire

21   Doing a project my own way

26   Being told I am needed

31   Completing a difficult task

36   Having an original idea

40   Being asked for help or advice

45   Giving advice to others based on past experience

51   Being needed

59   Having a daily plan

V. Doing: 8 Items

(Item Number/Item)

13   Doing volunteer work

20   Collecting recipes

27   Working on a community project

33   Baking because I feel creative

41   Bargain hunting

47   Arranging flowers

55   Creative crafts

62   Shopping for a new outfit

Scoring Option Number One: The "Eyeballing" Approach

Once you have received the client's responses, **IF** you do not elect to use the software program, then we recommend that you begin by eyeballing the responses: you should be looking for the **DISCREPANCY** between the frequency and pleasure ratings for each item and make note of the item number so that you can refer to it again. Several kinds of discrepancies are worth noting: (a) if frequency is 0 and pleasure (presumed pleasure) is rated 2 (which is high), then that suggests that if the client were able to do this activity, he would get pleasure from it; hence it is one to consider highly for inclusion in the individualized list (of activities to be increased). (b) If the frequency is 1 and pleasure is 2, this would indicate a low frequency item that also is a good candidate for being increased. On the other hand, if the frequency is 2 (high) and pleasure is 0, that would suggest an item to be decreased—although that is not the focus here (since you are trying to help the client generate a personalized list of everyday pleasant activities to INCREASE) the information may be useful at another point in the therapy.

Now, assuming you have marked (typically) 25 or 30 of the items with these kinds of discrepancies, you could review them and see how they cluster into the 5 categories described previously. For example, if 6 of the 8 socializing items are endorsed, that would be a strong indicator of the relevance of this domain for that individual. Since all people are different in what they consider pleasurable, it is worth the time and effort to study the COPPES and highlight those items of most relevance to this particular client. It is not necessary to group them into the categories we suggest; these can be helpful but we have used the scale on an item-by-item basis as well and it has worked just fine.

Next, you would share specific COPPES information with the client directly and discuss what items will be included on his list. This is an important step, since some items may simply be (or seem) impossible to increase for that individual at this time. For example, "meditating" may be an activity that the person says he would find very pleasurable but when you discuss it with him, you find he does not have a meditation practice established; this therefore may not be feasible at present—until the person has received some instruction in the practice and feels confident that it is something he CAN and WANTS TO do each day. That might become something that the person decides is a "project" he wants to do outside of therapy, that you could encourage him to undertake, but it would not be included on the daily tracking form. Items need to be discussed for practicality and likelihood of being able to be increased on an almost-daily basis in order to warrant inclusion.

The goal is to develop a daily tracking form of 10 potentially pleasant everyday activities that the client is likely to be able to increase. Therefore, the final step in this approach is to discuss **OBSTACLES** to doing these activities, and to engage in a problem-solving process to try and remove or reduce the obstacles. For example, if the client would enjoy "having a daily plan" but doesn't do that now, some possible obstacles would be: lack of time, belief that he is so poorly organized that he can't even develop a daily plan; having done it in the past but it didn't work, etc. This is grist for the therapeutic mill since, clearly, the activity will not be increased until the obstacles (in this case, thoughts about inadequacy and predicting future failures from past failures) are addressed. Doing this kind of problem solving as the list is being generated makes it much more realistic and allows for smooth integration of cognitive and behavioral elements of therapy.

Finally, then, there is an individual realistic list of activities for daily monitoring.

Therapist Note

■ *If it is not possible to generate 10 items (as we recommend in the manuals) or if the client is severely depressed, starting out with 5 or 6 is suggested (rather than abandoning this approach altogether). The list can always be added to, or changed, as new information becomes available. In fact, it should be updated regularly, and tracking should continue throughout therapy, for this intervention to have maximum impact. Be sure that the client understands this adage:* ■

Four Pleasant Events a Day Keeps the Blues Away

if they are Consciously Chosen and Deliberately Done

Pleasant events that just "happen" are only temporarily effective in improving mood; those that are consciously chosen, and deliberately done (i.e., planned into one's schedule) are much more effective for long-term improvement in affective states.

Scoring Option Number Two: The Computer Software Approach

The following information is necessary if you prefer to use the electronic scoring and graphing program. This program is free, but we ask you to contact us so that we can keep a record of who might be using the scale, and also inform you of any available updates.

Instructions for Using the COPPES Computer Software Program

Step 1
Launch your Internet web browser.

Step 2:
In the address bar, type in the web address for the Older Adult and Family Center:

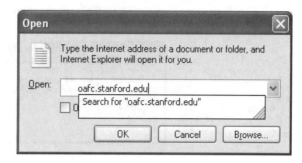

Step 3:

When the Older Adult and Family Center web page loads, click on the link for the COPPES (California Older Person's Pleasant Events Schedule) and follow the on-screen instructions to download and install the application.

Step 4:

By default, the application is installed in this folder on your hard drive: C:\Program Files\PES

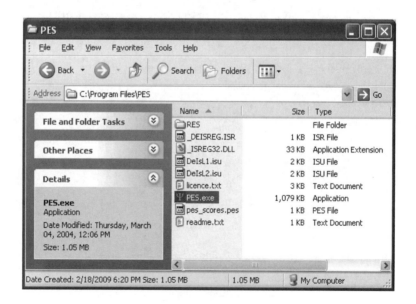

Double click on the PES.exe file to start the application.

Step 5:

When you start the COPPES application, it will ask for a password.

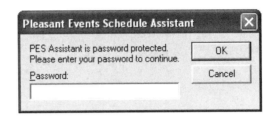

The password is: **ken**

Step 6:

We would appreciate your sending an e-mail message to **Dr. Ken Rider** so that we may have a record of who is using the program and we can correspond with you about updates, etc. Dr. Rider completed an exploratory and confirmatory factor analysis of data on approximately 600 participants, and then developed a program to score and graph data using the factors obtained on the normative sample. Scoring and interpretation of the computerized COPPES is included in a manual that is available from the Older Adult and Family Center Web site.

Dr. Rider's e-mail address is: **krider@pacbell.net**

Recommended Readings on the Use of CBT With Older Adults

Gallagher-Thompson, D., Steffen, A., & Thompson, L. W. (Editors). 2008. *Handbook of Behavioral and Cognitive Therapies with Older Adults*. NY: Springer.

Laidlaw, K., Thompson, L. W., Dick-Siskin, L., & Gallagher-Thompson, D. (2003). *Cognitive behaviour therapy with older people*. West Sussex, England: John Wiley & Sons.

Organista, K. C., & Muñoz, R. F. (1996). Cognitive behavioral therapy with Latinos. *Cognitive and Behavioral Practice, 3*, 255–270.

Persons, J. B., Davidson, J., & Tompkins, M. A. (2001). *Essential components of cognitive-behavior therapy for depression*. Washington, DC: American Psychological Association.

Rybarczyk, B., Gallagher-Thompson, D., Rodman, J., Zeiss, A., Gantz, F., & Yesavage, J. (1992). Applying cognitive-behavioral psychotherapy to the chronically ill elderly: Treatment issues and case illustrations. *International Psychogeriatrics, 4*, 127–140.

Thompson, L. W., & Gallagher, D. (1984). Efficacy of psychotherapy in the treatment of late-life depression. *Advances in Behaviour Research and Therapy, 6*, 127–139.

Wright, J. H., Basco, M., R., & Thase, M. E. (2006). *Learning cognitive-behavior therapy: An illustrated guide*. Washington, DC: American Psychiatric Publishing.

Homework/Home Practice Reading List

Coon, D. W., & Gallagher-Thompson, D. (2002). Encouraging homework completion among older adults in therapy. *Journal of Clinical Psychology/In Session: Psychotherapy in Practice, 58*, 549–563.

Coon, D. W., & Thompson, L. W. (2003). Association between homework compliance and treatment outcome among older adult outpatients with depression. *American Journal of Geriatric Psychiatry,* *11,* 53–61.

Coon, D. W., Thompson, L. W., & Gallagher-Thompson, D. (2007). Adapting homework for an older adult client with cognitive impairment. *Cognitive and Behavioral Practice, 14,* 252–260.

Coon, D. W., Thompson, L. W., Rabinowitz, Y. G., & Gallagher-Thompson, D. (2005). Older adults. In N. Kazantizis, F. P. Deane, K. R. Ronan, & L. L'Abate (Eds.), *Using homework assignments in cognitive-behavior therapy* (pp. 117–152). New York: Routledge Taylor & Francis Group.

Kazantzis, N., Deane, F. P., & Ronan, K. R. (2000). Homework assignments in cognitive and behavioral therapy: A meta-analysis. *Clinical Psychology: Science and Practice, 7,* 189–202.

Kazantzis, N., Pachana, N. A., & Secker, D. L. (2003). Cognitive-behavioral therapy for older adults: Practical guidelines for the use of homework assignments. *Cognitive and Behavioral Practice, 10,* 325–333.

Tompkins, M. A. (2002). Guidelines for enhancing homework compliance. *Journal of Clinical Psychology/In Session: Psychotherapy in Practice, 58,* 565–576.

Age-Related Changes in Psychological and Physiological Functioning

Birren, J. E., & Schaie, K., W. (Eds.). (2001). *Handbook of the psychology of aging* (5th ed.). San Diego: Academic Press.

Kane, R. L., Ouslander, J. G., Abrass, I. B., & Resnick, B. (2009). *Essentials of clinical geriatrics.* New York: McGraw Hill Medical.

Knopf, K. (2004). *Fitness over 50.* Winston-Salem, NC: Hunter Textbooks.

Federal Inter-Agency Forum on Aging-Related Statistics (website). (2006). Older Americans update 2006: Key indicators of well-being. Available online at http://www.AgingStats.gov.

National Center for Injury Prevention and Control. (2001). Falls and hip fractures among older adults. Available online at http://www.cdc.gov/ncipc/factsheets/falls.htm.

Robert Wood Johnson Foundation. (2001). National blueprint: Increasing physical activity among adults age 50 and older. *Journal of Aging and Physical Activity, 9,* S5–13.

Spirduso, W. W., Francis, R. J., & MacRae, P. G. (Eds.). (2005). *Physical dimensions of aging* (2nd ed.). Champaign, IL: Human Kinetics.

Woods, B. (2008). Normal and abnormal ageing. In K. Laidlaw & B. Knight (Eds.), *Handbook of Emotional disorders in later life: Assessment and Treatment* (pp. 33–58). Oxford, England: Oxford University Press.

National Resources for Older Adults

Organization Name	Brief Description	Contact Information
General Information		
Eldercare Locator—Area Agencies on Aging	Links older adults and their family members to state and local area agencies on aging (AAAs) and community-based organizations that help older adults remain at home and in the community.	Eldercare Hotline: (800) 677-1116 Available weekdays 9 a.m.–8 p.m. Spanish-speaking information specialist available. www.eldercare.gov
American Association of Retired Persons (AARP)	Provides information on a variety of issues including long-term care, retirement, financial and legal resources, etc.	(888) 687-2277 Available weekdays 7 a.m.–midnight ET. www.aarp.org
Health-Related Issues		
Alzheimer's Association	Provides information and care consultation on recognizing dementia, planning and paying for care, and linking local support and resources.	24 × 7 Hotline: (800) 272-3900 www.alz.org
Association for Frontotemporal Dementias (FTD)	Provides information and support to people with FTD and to their families.	(866) 507-7222 www.ftd-picks.org
Lewy Body Dementia Association, Inc.	Provides information and support to patients with Lewy body dementia (LBD) and to their families.	(800) 539-9767 www.lbda.org
American Cancer Society	The national call center provides information for cancer patients and their caregivers on community programs and services.	(800) 227-2345 www.cancer.org

continued

continued

Cancer Information, National Cancer Institute	Provides personalized, confidential responses to specific questions about cancer.	(800) 422-6237 Available weekdays 9 a.m.–4:30 p.m. EST. Spanish-speaking information specialists available. www.cancer.gov
American Chronic Pain Association	Offers resources for patients and their families to better manage chronic pain.	(800) 533-3231 www.theacpa.org
American Pain Foundation	Provides information on resources for patients with pain and their families.	(800) 615-7246 www.painfoundation.org
American Diabetes Association	Provides information on services to people with diabetes.	(800) 342-2383 Available weekdays 8:30 a.m.–8 p.m. EST. Spanish-speaking representative available. www.diabetes.org/
American Heart Association	Provides information on prevention and treatment of heart disease and stroke.	(800) 242-8721 www.americanheart.org
American Parkinson Disease Association, Inc.	Provides patient and caregiver support and referrals to local resources.	(800) 223-2732 www.apdaparkinson.org
Parkinson's Disease Foundation	The toll-free line answers questions regarding Parkinson's disease.	(800) 457-6676 www.pdf.org
American Stroke Association	Provides information and referrals to stroke survivors and their caregivers.	Stroke Family Warmline: (888) 478-7653 www.strokeassociation.org
National Stroke Association	Provides information and resources to stroke survivors and their families.	(800) 787-6537 www.stroke.org
Arthritis Foundation	Answers queries on arthritis-related information and provides linkages to community-based services to help with people suffering from arthritis.	(800) 283-7800 www.arthritis.org
Brain Injury Association of America	Offers a helpline providing information on brain injury and to assist families of brain injury patients seeking support.	(800) 444-6443 www.biausa.org

continued

Caring Connections	A program of the National Hospice and Palliative Care Organization that offers free resources and information on advance care, financial planning, and hospice care.	(800) 658-8898 Helpline in Spanish: (877) 658-8896 www.caringinfo.org
Hospice Foundation of America	Provides information about end-of-life care.	(800) 854-3402 Available weekdays 8:30 a.m.–5:30 p.m. EST. www.hospicefoundation.org
Hearing Loss Association of America	Provides information on healthcare, education, local support, and other resources for people with hearing loss.	(301) 657-2248 www.hearingloss.org
National Alcohol Substance Abuse Information Center (NASAIC)	Provides information on drug and alcohol addiction treatment facts and other related questions.	(800) 784-6776 Available 24 × 7. www.addictioncareoptions. com
National Alliance on Mental Illness	Offers a helpline that answers questions regarding mental health issues and links to local resources.	(800) 950-6264 www.nami.org
Senior Site—American Foundation for the Blind	Offers information and support to older adults and their families coping with age-related eye diseases, and helps to locate local services.	(800)232-5463 www.afb.org/seniorsite/

Health Insurance/Legal Services/Financial Planning

The Health Insurance Resource Center	Provides information on low-cost and affordable health insurance, health care, and hospice in each state.	(800) 798-8447 http://www.ahirc.org/
Housing Information for Seniors—U.S. Department of Housing & Urban Development	Provides information on housing options, financial assistance resources, and guides.	(202) 708-1112 www.hud.gov/groups/ seniors.cfm
Identity Theft Resource Center	Provides information to prevent and recover from identity theft.	(858) 693-7935 www.idtheftcenter.org
National Crime Prevention Council	Provides crime prevention and personal safety information for older Americans.	(202) 422-6272 www.ncpc.org

continued

continued

Medicare	The toll-free line offers information on Medicare and health plans available in your local areas.	(800) 633-4227 Available 24 × 7. Spanish-speaking customer service representative available. www.medicare.gov
Medicare Rights Center	Provides information on rights and benefits of Medicare, health plan options, and drug coverage.	Counseling Hotline: (800) 333-4114 Available weekdays 9 a.m.–1 p.m. ET. www.medicarerights.org
American Bar Association— Commission on Law and Aging	Provides linkages to legal services in each state.	(202) 662-8690 www.abanet.org/aging
National Academy of Elder Law Attorneys	Provides help to locate an elder law attorney who deals with legal issues affecting older adults.	(520) 881-4005 www.naela.org
National Legal Aid & Defender Association	Provides linkages to local attorneys for people in need of legal assistance.	(202) 452-0620 www.nlada.org
Patient Advocate Foundation	Provides mediation between patients and their employers and/or creditors to resolve insurance, job retention, and/or debt crisis relating to the patient's condition.	(800) 532-5274 www.patientadvocate.org
Federal Citizen Information Center	Answers questions about federal programs, benefits, and services.	(800) 333-4636 www.pueblo.gsa.gov/call/ ncc.htm
Social Security	Provides information on benefits and other services, and retirement planning.	(800) 772-1213 Social Security representative available weekdays 7 a.m.–7 p.m. www.ssa.gov
Society of Certified Senior Advisors (CSA)	Helps with locating a CSA and provides information on issues relating to older adults' health, housing, and finances.	(800) 653-1785 www.society-csa.com

continued

Caregiving Resources		
National Center on Caregiving at Family Caregiver Alliance	Has a national hotline that provides informational assistance to family caregivers in the United States.	(800) 445-8106 Available weekdays 9 a.m.–5 p.m. PT. www.caregiver.org
National Family Caregiver Association	Provides support, information, and referral services to family caregivers.	(800) 896-3650 www.nfcacares.org
Well Spouse Association	Provides support for any spouse or partner caring for someone who is chronically ill or disabled.	(800) 838-0879 www.wellspouse.org
Other Resources		
Safe Driving for Older Adults—U.S. Department of Transportation	Provides information about traffic and auto safety for older adults.	Auto Safety Hotline: (888) 327-4236 http://www.nhtsa.dot.gov/ people/injury/olddrive/ OlderAdultswebsite/
National Center on Elder Abuse	Provides links to local helplines to report elder abuse, neglect, or exploitation.	(202) 898-2586 www.ncea.aoa.gov
National Long-Term Care Ombudsman Resource Center	Provides information on the role of ombudsman in helping nursing home residents and their families and helps to locate local ombudsman services.	(202) 232-2275 www.ltcombudsman.org
Nursing Home Compare	A government resource providing information on the past performances of every Medicare- and Medicaid-certified nursing home in the state.	(800) 633-4227 www.medicare.gov/ NHCompare/home.asp
National Center on Senior Transportation	Offers a hotline that answers questions regarding transportation services for older adults.	(866) 528-6278 Available weekdays 9 a.m.–5 p.m. EST. www.seniortransportation.net

continued

continued

National Suicide Prevention Lifeline	Provides suicide-prevention service to anyone in suicidal crisis.	(800) 273-8255 (Veterans press 1) Spanish Lifeline: (888) 628-9454 www.suicidepreventionlifeline. org
The Compassionate Friends	Offers assistance to bereaved parents, siblings, grandparents, and other family members during the natural grieving process after a child dies.	(877) 969-0010 www.compassionatefriends.org

References

Arfken, C. I., Lichtenberg, P. A., & Tancer, M. E. (1999). Cognitive impairment and depression predict mortality in medically ill older adults. *Journal of Gerontology, A: Biological Sciences and Medical Sciences, 54,* M152–M156.

Beck, A. T. (1976). *Cognitive therapy and the emotional disorders.* New York: International Universities Press.

Beck, A. T., Kovacs, M., & Weissman, A. (1979). Assessment of suicidal intention: The scale for suicidal ideation. *Journal of Consulting and Clinical Psychology, 47,* 343–352.

Beck, A. T., & Steer, R. A. (1993). *Hopelessness Scale Manual.* San Antonio, TX: The Psychological Corporation.

Beck, A. T., Steer, R. A., & Brown, G. K. (1996). *Manual for the Beck Depression Inventory* (2nd ed.). San Antonio, TX: The Psychological Corporation.

Beck, A. T., Steer, R. A., Kovacs, M., & Garrison, B. (1985, May). Hopelessness and eventual ***suicide***: A 10-year prospective study of patients hospitalized with suicidal ideation. *American Journal of Psychiatry, 142*(5), 559–563.

Beck, A. T., Rush, J., Shaw, B., et al. (1979). *Cognitive therapy of depression* (p. 425). New York: Guilford Press.

Beck, J. (1995). *Cognitive therapy, basics and beyond.* New York: Guilford Press.

Bellak, L., & Small, L. (1965). *Emergency psychotherapy and brief psychotherapy.* New York: Grune & Stratton.

Bernstein, D. A., Carlson, C. R., & Schmidt, J. E. (2007). Progressive relaxation: Abbreviated methods. In P. M. Lehrer, R. L. Woolfolk, & W. E. Sime (Eds.), *Principles and practice of stress management* (pp. 88–122). New York: Guilford Press.

Birren, J. E., & Schaie, W. K. (2005). *Handbook of the psychology of aging* (6th ed.). New York: Academic Press.

Black, S. A., & Markides, K. S. (1999). Depressive symptoms and mortality in older Mexican Americans. *Annals of Epidemiology, 9*, 45–52.

Blazer, D. G. (2003). Depression in late life: Review and commentary. *Journal of Gerontology: Medical Sciences, 58A*, 249–265.

Blazer, D. G., Steffens, D. C., & Busse, E. W. (2007). *Essentials of geriatric psychiatry*. Washington, DC: American Psychiatric Publishing, Inc.

Blow, F., Brower, K. J., Schulenberg, J. E., Demo-Dananberg, L. M., Young, J. P., & Beresford, T. P. (1992). The Michigan alcoholism screening test—geriatric version (MAST-G): A new elderly-specific screening instrument. *Alcoholism: Clinical and Experimental Research, 16*, 372–376.

Blow, F. C., Gillespie, B. W., Barry, K. L., et al. (1998). Brief screening for alcohol problems in elderly populations using the Short Michigan Alcoholism Screening Test—Geriatric Version (SMAST-G). *Alcoholism: Clinical and Experimental Research, 22* (Suppl.), 131A.

Bruce, M. L., Ten Have, T. R., Reynolds, C. F., et al. (2004). Reducing suicidal ideation and depressive symptoms in depressed older primary care patients: A randomized controlled trial. *Journal of the American Medical Association, 291*, 1081–1091.

Burns, D. D. (1999). *The feeling good handbook*. Revised edition. New York: Penguin Publishing Group.

Center for Substance Abuse Treatment. (1998). Substance abuse among older adults (TIP Series #26). DHHS Publication No. (SMA): 02-3688. Rockville, MD: Substance Abuse and Mental Health Services Administration.

Center for Substance Abuse Treatment. (2006). Pocket Screening Instruments for Health Care and Social Service Providers. DHHS Publication accessed September 15, 2008. http://kap.samhsa.gov/products/manuals/tips/index.htm.

Centers for Disease Control and Prevention "WISQARS Injury Mortality Reports, 1999–2006" (Database Query) Accessed May 11, 2009 http://webappa.cdc.gov/sasweb/ncipc/mortrate10_sy.html.

Centers for Disease Control and Prevention "Facts at a Glance: Suicide" Summer 2008 http://www.cdc.gov/ViolencePrevention/pdf/Suicide-DataSheet-a.pdf.

Cheavens, J. S., & Lynch, T. R. (2008). Dialectical behavior therapy for personality disorders in older adults. In D. Gallagher-Thompson, A. M. Steffen, & L. W. Thompson (Eds.), *Handbook of behavioral and cognitive therapies with older adults* (pp. 187–199). New York: Springer Publishing Co.

Clifford, P. A., Cipher, D. J., Roper, K. D., Snow, A. L., & Molinari, V. (2008). Cognitive behavioral pain management interventions for long-term care residents with physical and cognitive disabilities. In D. Gallagher-Thompson, A. Steffen, & L. W. Thompson (Eds.), *Handbook of behavioral and cognitive therapies with older adults* (pp. 76–101). New York: Springer Publishing Co.

Covinsky, K. E., Kahana, E., Chin, M. H., et al. (1999). Depressive symptoms and 3-year mortality in older hospitalized medical patients. *Annals of Internal Medicine, 130,* 563–569.

Crits-Christoph, P., Baranackie, K., Kurcias, J. S., Beck, A. T., et al., (1991). Meta-analysis of therapist effects in psychotherapy outcome studies. *Psychotherapy Research, 1,* 81–91.

Crum, R. M., Anthony, J. C., Bassett, S. S., & Folstein, M. F. (1993). Population-based norms for the Mini-Mental State Examination by age and educational level. *Journal of the American Medical Association (JAMA), 269*(18), 2386–2391.

Edelstein, B. A., Woodhead, E. L., Segal, D. L., Heisel, M. J., Bower, E. H., Lowery, A. J., & Stoner, S. A. (2008). Older adult psychological assessment: Current instrument status and related considerations. *Clinical Gerontologist, 31*(3), 1–35.

Fiske, A., O'Riley, A. A., & Widoe, R. K. (2008). Physical health and suicide in late life: An evaluative review. *Clinical Gerontologist, 31*(4), 31–50.

Folstein, M. F., Folstein, S. E., & McHugh, P. R (1975). Mini-mental state. *Journal of Psychiatric Research, 12,* 189–198.

Frank, E., Frank, N., & Comes, C. (1993). Interpersonal psychotherapy in the treatment of late life depression. In G. Klerman & M. Weissman (Eds.), *New applications of interpersonal psychotherapy.* Washington, DC: American Psychiatric Press.

Frank, E., & Spanier, C. (1995). Interpersonal psychotherapy for depression: Overview, clinical efficacy and future directions. *Clinical Psychology, Science and Practice, 2,* 349–365.

Gallagher-Thompson, D., Gray, H., Tang, P., Pu, C.-Y., Tse, C., Hsu, S., Leung, L., Wang, P., Kwo, E., Tong, H.-Q., Long, J., & Thompson, L. W. (2007). Impact of in-home intervention versus telephone support in reducing depression and stress of Chinese caregivers: Results of a pilot study. *American Journal of Geriatric Psychiatry, 15,* 425–434.

Gallagher-Thompson, D., Steffen, A., & Thompson, L. W. (Editors). 2008. *Handbook of Behavioral and Cognitive Therapies with Older Adults.* NY: Springer.

Gallagher-Thompson, D., Wang, P-C., Liu, W., Cheung, V., Peng, R., China, D., & Thompson, L. W. (In press). Effectiveness of a psychoeducational skill training DVD program to reduce stress in Chinese American dementia caregivers. *Aging and Mental Health.*

Gallagher-Thompson, D., Gray, H. L., Dupart, T., Jimenez, D., & Thompson, L. W. (2008). Effectiveness of cognitive/behavioral small group intervention for reduction of depression and stress in Non Hispanic White and Hispanic/Latino women dementia family caregivers: Outcomes and mediators of change. *Journal of Rational-Emotive and Cognitive-Behavior Therapy, 26,* 286–303.

Gallagher-Thompson, D., Coon, D. W., Solano, N., Ambler, C., Rabinowitz, Y., & Thompson, L. W. (2003). Change in indices of distress among Latina and Anglo female caregivers of elderly relatives with dementia: Site specific results from the REACH national collaborative study. *The Gerontologist, 43*(4), 580–591.

Gallagher-Thompson, D., Arean, P., Rivera, P., & Thompson, L. W. (2001). A psychoeducational intervention to reduce distress in Hispanic family caregivers: Results of a pilot study. *Clinical Gerontologist, 23*(1/2), 17–32.

Gallagher-Thompson, D., Hanley-Peterson, P., & Thompson, L. (1990). Maintenance of gains versus relapse following brief psychotherapy for depression. *Journal of Consulting and Clinical Psychology, 58*(3), 371–374.

Gallagher, D. E., & Thompson, L. W. (1981). *Depression in the elderly: A behavioral treatment manual.* Los Angeles: University of Southern California Press.

Gallagher, D. E., & Thompson, L. W. (1982). Treatment of major depressive disorder in older adult outpatients with brief psychotherapies. *Psychotherapy: Theory, Research and Practice, 19*(4), 482–490.

Greenberger, D., & Padesky, C. A. (1995). *Mind over mood: Change how you feel by changing the way you think.* New York: Guilford Press.

Haber, D. (2007). *Health promotion and aging.* New York: Springer Publishing.

Hays, P., & Iwamasa, G. (2006). *Culturally responsive cognitive-behavioral therapy.* Washington, DC: American Psychological Association Publications.

Heisel, M. J., & Flett, G. L. (2006). The development and initial validation of the Geriatric Suicide Ideation Scale. *The American Journal of Geriatric Psychiatry, 14,* 742–751.

Heisel, M. J., & Flett, G. L. (2008). Psychological resilience to suicide ideation among older adults. *Clinical Gerontologist, 31*(4), 51–70.

Horowitz, M., & Kaltreider, N. (1979). Brief Psychotherapy of the stress response. *Psychiatric Clinics of North America, 2*, 365–378.

Kane, R., Ouslander, J., Abrass, I., & Resnick, B. (2008). *Essentials of clinical geriatrics* (6th ed.). New York: McGraw-Hill.

Keller, M. B., Laver, P., Friedman, B., et al. (1987). The Longitudinal Interval Follow-up Evaluation: A comprehensive method for assessing outcome in prospective longitudinal studies. *Archives of General Psychiatry, 44*, 540–548.

Knopf, K. G. (2004). *Principles of fitness therapy.* Winston-Salem, NC: Hunter Textbooks, Inc.

Koenig, H. G., & Blazer, D. G. (2007). In D. G. Blazer, D. C. Steffens, & E. W. Busse, (Eds.), *Essentials of geriatric psychiatry* (pp. 145–176). Washington, DC: American Psychiatric Publishing, Inc.

Laidlaw, K., Thompson, L. W., Dick-Siskin, L., & Gallagher-Thompson, D. (2003). *Cognitive behaviour therapy with older people.* Chichester, England: John Wiley & Sons.

Laidlaw, K., Davidson, K., Toner, H., Jackson, G., Clark, S., Cross, S., et al. (2008). A randomized controlled trial of cognitive behavior therapy *vs* treatment as usual in the treatment of mild to moderate late life depression. *International Journal of Geriatric Psychiatry, 23*, 843–850.

Lewinsohn, P. M., Munoz, R. F., Youngren, M. A., & Zeiss, A. M. (1986). *Control your depression: Revised and updated* (2nd ed.). New York: Prentice Hall Press.

Lewinsohn, P. M., Hoberman, H., Teri, L., et al. (1985). An integrative theory of depression. In S. Reiss & R. R. Bootzin (Eds.), *Theoretical issues in behavior therapy* (pp. 331–359). New York: Academic Press.

Lezak, M. D. (1995). *Neuropsychological assessment* (3rd ed.). New York: Oxford University Press.

Lowe, P. A., & Reynolds, C. R. (2006). Examination of the psychometric properties of the Adult Manifest Anxiety Scale—Elderly Version scores. *Educational and Psychological Measurement, 66*(1), 93–115.

Marmar, C. R., Horowitz, M. J., Weiss, D. S., Wilner, N. R., & Kaltreider, N. B. (1988). A controlled trial of brief psychotherapy and mutual-help group treatment of conjugal bereavement. *American Journal of Psychiatry, 145*, 203–209.

Murphy, E., Smith, R., Lindsay, J., et al. (1988). Increased mortality rates in late-life depression. *British Journal of Psychiatry, 152*, 347–353.

Pachana, N., Byrne, G., Siddle, H., Koloski, N., Harley, E., & Arnold, E. (2006). Development and validation of the Geriatric Anxiety Inventory. *International Psychogeriatrics, 19*, 103–114.

Powers, D. V., Thompson, L. W., & Gallagher-Thompson, D. (2008). The benefits of using psychotherapy skills following treatment for depression: An examination of "afterwork" and a test of the skills hypothesis in older adults. *Cognitive and Behavioral Practice, 15*, 194–202.

Radloff, L. S. (1977). The CES-D: A self-report depression scale for research in the general population. *Applied Psychological Measurement, 1*, 385–401.

Reynolds, C. R., Richmond, B. O., & Lowe, P. A. (2003). *Adult manifest anxiety scale—elderly version.* Los Angeles: Western Psychological Services.

Rovner, B. W., German, P. S., Brant, L. J., et al. (1991). Depression and mortality in nursing homes. *JAMA, 265*, 993–996.

Rowe, J. R., & Kahn, R. L. (1998). *Successful aging.* New York: Pantheon Books.

Rush, A. J., Jr., First, M. B., & Blacker, D. (Eds.). (2008). *Handbook of psychiatric measures.* Washington, DC: American Psychiatric Publishing, Inc.

Scogin, F., Morthland, M., Kaufman, A., Burgio, L., Chaplin, W., & Kong, G. (2007). Improving quality of life in diverse rural older adults: A randomized trial of a psychological treatment. *Psychology and Aging, 22*, 657–665.

Spirduso, W. W., Francis, K. L., & MacRae, P. G. (2005). *Physical dimensions of aging* (2nd ed.). Champaign, IL: Human Kinetics.

Thompson, L. W., (1996) Cognitive-Behavioral Therapy and Treatment for Late-Life Depression. *Journal of Clinical Psychiatry, 57* (supplement 5), 29–37.

Thompson, L. W., Spira, A. P., Depp, C. A., McGee, J. S., & Gallagher-Thompson, D. (2006). The geriatric caregiver. In M. E. Agronin & G. J. Maletta (Eds.), *Principles and practice of geriatric psychiatry* (pp. 37–48). Philadelphia, PA: Lippincott Williams & Wilkins.

Thompson, L. W., Kaye, J. L., Tang, P. C. Y., & Gallagher-Thompson, D. (2004). Bereavement and adjustment disorders. In D. Blazer, D. Steffens & E. Busse (Eds.), *Textbook of Geriatric Psychiatry, 3rd ed.* Chapter 19, (pp. 319–338). Washington, D.C.: American Psychiatric Press.

Thompson, L. W., McGee, J. S., & Gallagher-Thompson, D. (2005). Cognitive behavioral therapy. Included in Geriatric Psychiatry section, entry 51.4i. In B. J. Sadock & V. A. Sadock (Eds.), *Comprehensive textbook of psychiatry, Vol. II, 8th edition.* (pp. 3758–3763). Philadelphia, PA: Lippincott, Williams & Wilkins.

Thompson, L. W., Powers, D. V., Coon, D. W., Takagi, K., McKibbin, C., & Gallagher-Thompson, D. (2000). Older adults. In J. R. White & A. S. Freeman (Eds.), *Cognitive-behavioral group therapy for specific problems and populations*. Chapter 9, (pp. 235–261). Washington, D.C.: American Psychological Association.

Thompson, L. W., Coon, D. W., Gallagher-Thompson, D., Sommer, B., & Koin, D. (2001). Comparison of desipramine and cognitive behavioral therapy in the treatment of elderly outpatients with mild to moderate depression. *American Journal of Geriatric Psychiatry, 9*(3), 225–240.

Thompson, L. W., Gallagher, D., & Breckenridge, J. S. (1987). Comparative effectiveness of psychotherapies for depressed elders. *Journal of Consulting and Clinical Psychology, 55*(3), 385–390.

Tombaugh, T. N., & McIntyre, N. J. (1992). The mini-mental state examination: A comprehensive review. *Journal of the American Geriatrics Society, 40*, 922–935.

Tuokko, H., Hadjistavropoulos, T., Miller, J. A., & Beattie, B. L. (1992). The clock test: A sensitive measure to differentiate normal elderly from those with Alzheimer's disease. *Journal of the American Geriatrics Society, 40*, 579–584.

Tuokko, H., Hadjistavropoulos, T., Miller, J. A., Horton, A., & Beattie, B. L. (1995). *The clock test: Administration and scoring manual*. Toronto, ON: Multi-Health Systems.

U.S. Census Bureau. (2001). *An aging world: 2001*. http://www.census.gov/prod/2001pubs/p95-01-1.pdf.

Yesavage, J., Brink, T. L., Rose, T. L., Lum, O., Huang, V., Adey, M., & Leirer, V. O., (1983). Development and validation of a geriatric depression screening scale: a preliminary report. *Journal of Psychiatric Research, 17*(1), 37–49.

Young, J., Klosko, J. S., & Weishaar, M. E. (2003). *Schema therapy: A practitioner's guide*. New York: Guilford Press.

Woods, B. (2008). Normal and abnormal ageing. In K. Laidlaw & B. Knight (Eds.), *Handbook of Emotional disorders in later life: Assessment and Treatment* (pp. 33–58). Oxford, England: Oxford University Press.

Wright, J. H., Basco, M. R., & Thase, M. E. (2006). *Learning cognitive-behavior therapy: An illustrated guide*. Washington, DC: American Psychiatric Publishing, Inc.

About the Authors

Dolores Gallagher-Thompson, PhD, ABPP, is Professor of Research in the Department of Psychiatry and Behavioral Sciences, Stanford University School of Medicine, Stanford, CA. She is also Director of the Stanford Geriatric Education Center there, which focuses on training clinicians in mental health and health issues specific to ethnically and culturally diverse older adults and their families. Currently, Dr. Gallagher-Thompson specializes in two complementary areas of research and clinical practice: older clients experiencing late-life depression, and family caregivers of relatives suffering from Alzheimer's disease (or another form of dementia). She has conducted research on these topics for over 20 years, with funding from the National Institute of Mental Health, National Institute on Aging, and the national office of the Alzheimer's Association. Specifically, her research has focused on developing and evaluating various psychological interventions to reduce depression and stress: For many years, she conducted studies on the efficacy of CBT for unipolar depression in both geriatric outpatients and in family caregivers. In the last decade, she has specialized primarily in intervention research with culturally diverse family caregivers, including African Americans, Hispanic/Latino Americans, and Asian Americans. She was Principal Investigator at the Palo Alto, CA, site of the REACH national collaborative research programs (Resources for Enhancing Alzheimer Caregivers Health); has developed a DVD and workbook in Chinese (based on CBT principles and techniques) to reduce distress in Chinese caregivers; and is now funded to develop a *fotonovela* in Spanish to teach CBT methods for reducing distress in Latino dementia caregivers. To her credit, she has about 200 publications in journals such as *Psychology and Aging*, the *Gerontologist*, and the *American Journal of Geriatric Psychiatry*, as well as having authored, coauthored, or edited five books. She is also co-editor-in-chief of the journal *Clinical Gerontologist* (along with Larry Thompson). Finally, Dr. Gallagher-Thompson is an active member of the Committee on Aging of the American Psychological Association, is a Fellow of Divisions 12 and 20, and is very active in a volunteer capacity with the local chapter of the Alzheimer's Association, where she helped to establish their multicultural outreach committee.

Larry W. Thompson, PhD, is an Emeritus Professor from the Department of Medicine, Stanford University School of Medicine, Stanford, CA, and first Goldman Family Professor at the Pacific Graduate School of Psychology, Palo Alto, CA. He is also president of a small psychological consulting firm based in Los Altos, CA. He has been at the forefront of research evaluating the use of cognitive-behavioral therapy (CBT) in the treatment of mood disorders in the elderly. During the course of his work he has developed and evaluated modifications of CBT to improve its efficacy in the treatment of older adults suffering from unipolar and bipolar depression. Over the past quarter century, he has trained graduate students in clinical psychology, social work, nursing, and related fields, as well as postdoctoral fellows in psychiatry, behavioral medicine, and psychology, in the application of CBT for the treatment of mood disorders in older adults. Together with colleagues, he has written or edited five books dealing with innovations in therapies for older adults. He has also been involved in the development and evaluation of several psychoeducational programs based on CBT principles to use with community groups interested in working on specific stressful problems, such as "how to improve life satisfaction," "dealing with frustration when caring for a mentally impaired spouse," "how to deal with the changing values and beliefs in the world," and so on. He has published over 150 articles in journals dealing with age-related health and mental health issues.